PUB W
IN
Hertfordshire

THIRTY CIRCULAR WALKS
AROUND HERTFORDSHIRE INNS

Alan Charles

COUNTRYSIDE BOOKS
NEWBURY, BERKSHIRE

COUNTRYSIDE BOOKS
3 Catherine Road
Newbury, Berkshire

ISBN 1 85306 294 4

Designed by Mon Mohan
Cover illustration by Colin Doggett
Photographs and maps by the author

Produced through MRM Associates Ltd., Reading
Typeset by Paragon Typesetters, Queensferry, Clwyd
Printed in England

Often and often it came back again
To mind, the day I passed the horizon ridge
To a new country, the path I had to find
By half-gaps that were stiles once in the hedge,
The pack of scarlet clouds running across
The harvest evening that seemed endless then
And after, and the inn where all were kind . . .

Edward Thomas
Over the Hills

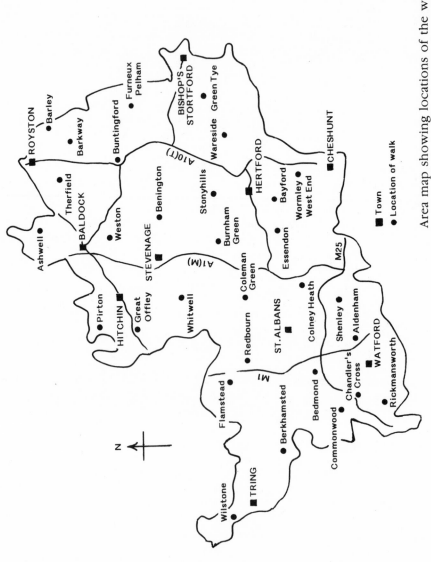

Area map showing locations of the walks.

Contents

Publisher's Note

We hope that you obtain considerable enjoyment from this book; great care has been taken in its preparation. However, changes of landlord and actual closures are sadly not uncommon. Likewise, although at the time of publication all routes followed public rights of way or well-established permitted paths, diversion orders can be made and permissions withdrawn.

We cannot accept responsibility for any inaccuracies, but we are anxious that all details covering both pubs and walks are kept up to date, and would therefore welcome information from readers which would be relevant to future editions.

Introduction

A glance at a map of Hertfordshire might lead you to the conclusion that this is a county with more than its fair share of major highways, and as such cannot be an area in which to find peace and tranquillity. While this is true in some parts of the county, there remains mile upon mile of delightful countryside where it is possible to 'get away from it all' and, better still, where quiet country walks can be enjoyed. When, as in this book, such walks are based on good country pubs, the walker's pleasure is complete.

The 30 pubs featured here have my seal of approval, I have tried and tested them all! Many were recommended by friends and casual acquaintances (my thanks to all of you) while others were discovered by chance. In the main they have been chosen for atmosphere, for quality of food and for price (pubs selling expensive bar food have been avoided). Not being an expert in the liquid arts I have to confess that the quality of the ales has not figured very largely in my choice. I have simply listed the brews that are on offer.

Many of the walks give access to other (mostly untried) pubs along the way. Where space allows these are shown symbolically on the sketch maps. They could be used as alternatives to the featured pubs – or as additions if it's a hot and thirsty day!

Most pubs are open for drinking during what I have called 'normal' hours. Give or take half an hour at each end, these are 11 am to 2.30 pm and 6 pm to 11 pm Monday to Saturday. Sunday opening hours are restricted by law to 12 noon to 3 pm and 7 pm to 10.30 pm. I have given actual opening times only when they differ significantly from the norm.

Lunchtime food is usually available between 12 noon and 2 to 2.30 pm. For evenings a popular 'sitting' is 7 pm to 9 or 9.30 pm. There are numerous variations on this: for example, some pubs serve meals lunchtimes only; many do not serve meals on Sunday evenings, while others serve no food at all on Sundays.

Some licensees are perfectly happy for customers who buy drinks to bring their own food and to eat this in the garden. There are others who merely tolerate the practice, and yet others who are strongly opposed. While I have mentioned those pubs where the practice is clearly welcomed, it is advisable to make absolutely certain before opening your lunchbox, especially if you are in a party all expecting to eat DIY.

Proposed changes in the law relating to children in pubs would, if instituted, enable licensees to admit those under 14 into their bars.

Since conditions will constantly change as more and more pubs are granted the appropriate licence, comments such as 'children can only be taken into the garden' should not be taken as the last word on the subject.

All of the pubs in this book have their own car parks, and all of the licensees are happy for customers to leave their cars while on the walk – but it would be polite to ask first.

Bus routes given in the text are only those which provide reasonably frequent links to main line railway stations – which are in turn linked to London's termini. Hertfordshire County Council publish a set of four timetables giving all services (including rail) in the county. These useful volumes can be obtained from public libraries or from railway stations, bus stations and council offices.

The walks average about 4½ miles in length and should take about 2 to 2½ hours to complete. The distances given are as measured from the map and do not allow for the extra ground trodden when walking uphill or downhill. Most of the walks are covered by the 1:50 000 Landranger series Ordnance Survey map 166, with the remainder on maps 153, 154, 165, 167 and 176. These maps are invaluable to the walker since they are clearly marked with public rights of way.

Compass bearings are given throughout the text as an aid to navigation. These bearings can be very useful in woodland or where there are no permanent points of reference. Having purchased your compass all you need is a few minutes' practice in using it. Another useful instrument is a walking stick. Since nettles and briars can quickly take over a footpath, this can be a valuable weapon in your defence.

Enjoy the walks; enjoy the pubs!

Alan Charles

MAP SYMBOLS

Described route along a path or track:

Described route along a road or metalled drive:

Other paths or tracks:
(not necessarily public rights of way)

Steep hill: Bridge:

Public house: Church:

River: R.ASH   R.RIB

House or other building: ☐ Town or village:

Golf course: ⊢   Car park: P

Woodland: Pond or lake:

Aerial mast: Railway:

① Rickmansworth
The Coach and Horses

This is a beautifully refurbished Greene King pub, attractive inside and out. With the pleasant atmosphere and the attention and care of the staff, it is simply a very pleasant place to be. Apart from the popular and tasty steak and Abbot Ale pie, the selection of main meals changes from day to day. Examples are chicken and mushroom pie, tuna lasagne and lamb rogan josh. Lighter meals include ploughman's, salads and jacket potatoes. These, along with the main meals, are available every lunchtime and evening except Sunday evening.

Not surprisingly, real ales are from the Greene King brewery – Rayments BBA, Abbot Ale and IPA. Drinking hours are normal. Children may join you in the upper level of the pub if having a meal, or outside on one of the two patios. Dogs are not welcome inside. Telephone: 01923 772433.

How to get there: The Coach and Horses is situated along the eastern half of the one-way High Street (the half with few shops). If you are driving to the pub, follow the 'Town Centre' signpost from the A412 roundabout adjacent to Rickmansworth Catholic church. There is a frequent train service from London on the Metropolitan line of

London Underground. Turn right out of Rickmansworth station and go downhill under the railway into Station Road; then turn left at the bottom into High Street and follow this right through past the shops and the Watersmeet Centre.

Parking: In the pub's own car park or in the free public car park opposite.

Length of the walk: 4¼ miles. Map: OS Landranger 176 West London Area and 166 Luton, Hertford and surrounding area (GR 062945).

This interesting figure of eight walk is almost equally divided between the towpath of the Grand Union Canal from Batchworth and the track bed of the disused Watford to Rickmansworth railway. The top of the '8' is linked by a path crossing Common Moor, a Site of Special Scientific Interest. Model aircraft enthusiasts are allowed to use part of the moor at certain times. If you wish to avoid them (and their noise) walk on Monday or Friday, or on Sunday afternoon. Since there are no hills or stiles, this walk is suitable for pushchairs, but it could be a bumpy ride!

The Walk

From the Coach and Horses cross High Street to Talbot Road opposite (not the adjacent works road). Be wary of fast traffic as you cross, High Street is one-way. Passing to the left of a public car park, follow Talbot Road over the Town Ditch; then go right with the road alongside the ditch and between numerous handsome cottages. Do not walk the whole length of the road but turn left into a small car park and over another road to Church Street, where you will be facing the church itself.

Turn left in Church Street and follow the curve of the road to the A404 roundabout and forward to the Batchworth canal bridge. A flight of steps on the left will lead you down to the Grand Union Canal towpath. The building just here was once the Boat Inn and had two licences, one for road level and one for canal level! Attached to this is the Batchworth Canal Centre – a worthwhile diversion.

Another worthwhile diversion is to have lunch or tea on *Albert*, a narrowboat moored here on the canal. One of the original fleet of Ovaltine boats, *Albert* was restored from a very derelict condition by enthusiast Chris Collins working single-handed. It is now a restaurant and tour boat.

To stay on the Grand Union towpath you will need to cross the metal bridge (numbered 172) adjacent to the canal centre. This bridge is above the canalised river Chess where it joins the Grand Union. The main flow from the Chess descends a weir and passes behind the centre. Conversion of the river Chess to a canal between Batchworth

11

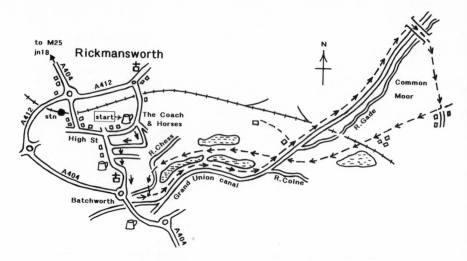

and Rickmansworth provided a link between the Grand Union and the town's brewery and gasworks. After about 200 yards you will be making a half-left turn along with the canal. The branch flowing from the opposite bank at this point once fed the wheels of Batchworth Mill, now a water company's pumping station.

In less than ½ mile the extensive waters of Sabey's Pool (a flooded gravel working) makes its appearance through the trees on the left; and soon after this the rivers Colne and Gade join the canal. Having now seen the rivers Chess, Colne and Gade in close proximity you will understand why the local administrative district of Three Rivers is so called.

The steel bridge spanning the canal between the points of entry of the two rivers is included on our return route. It is a remnant of the Watford to Rickmansworth railway which closed to passengers in 1952 and to freight in 1967.

You will soon pass Lot Mead House and lock, where a track runs left to the medieval Croxley Tithe Barn, which was restored by the County Council. Another 250 yards will see you under a busy railway bridge carrying trains from London to Amersham and Aylesbury. Beyond the bridge a stretch of magnificent wild scrub accompanies the towpath. Underneath these plants (much favoured by birds and insects) lie years of rubbish from London's underground stations – replacing gravel extracted for the construction of Wembley Stadium.

On arrival at the next lock (⅔ mile from the previous railway bridge), cross both the canal and the river Gade and strike half-right across Common Moor (180°). This will take you in the direction of a distant wooded escarpment (Moor Park Golf Course) and on to the track bed of the former Watford to Rickmansworth railway on the far side of the moor. Turn right in the track bed (there are houses nearby) and commence your 1½ mile walk back to Rickmansworth. In the process you will pass under a railway bridge, then between marshes and lakes before recrossing the canal.

Towards the end of that 1½ mile stretch and while walking under tall trees, you will cross an arm of the river Chess followed by the canalised Chess itself. You should ignore a bridge on the left soon after this and go forward to a tarmacked parking area. Turn left here and left again towards – but not across – a drawbridge, and right into a narrow paved path alongside a builder's merchant's yard. This will take you to a footbridge and back to the Grand Union Canal.

Go right in the road at the bridge and forward to Church Street. By way of a change you could stay in Church Street and turn right into High Street at the main crossing. Alternatively (retracing your earlier steps, but in reverse) turn right into a rough drive immediately beyond Church Terrace. Soon cross a road to a short path and then right in Talbot Road, following this back to the pub.

② Chandler's Cross
The Clarendon Arms

If you pass this way often, you will be aware of the puns regularly chalked on a blackboard outside the Clarendon Arms. There is something to suit every occasion: the Test Match, Father's Day, the state of the weather – or whatever. If you go inside and meet the folk beyond the puns, you will find them friendly and courteous. This, and the good food and drink, make the Clarendon Arms a very pleasant pub.

You can eat here any day of the week, lunchtime or evening. On Sunday the choice is reduced somewhat; but since it sometimes includes the very popular (and very tasty) Clarendon Pie, you can't go far wrong. The regular menu (Monday to Saturday) includes that same pie, also fish of the day, chicken, chilli, fresh pasta, omelettes, jacket potatoes, ploughman's and sandwiches.

Since this is a freehouse it can be choosy about its real ales. The regulars are Ruddles County and Marston's Bitter, with other brews appearing from time to time. Those concerned about their alcohol intake could opt for the low-priced low-alcohol lager or the unlimited coffee. Drinking hours are normal except for an earlier than average opening time of 5 pm Monday to Friday.

Children are welcome, but if you take them on to the patio at the

front (there is no garden) they will need your watchful eye. Dogs are not permitted inside, but are welcome on the patio – where bowls are provided.
Telephone: 01923 262924.

How to get there: Chandler's Cross is 2 miles north-west of Watford as the crow flies. A picturesque approach is via Grove Mill Lane. Join the lane from the A411 one mile north-west of Watford. Turn first left into Fir Tree Hill after 1¼ miles and drive a further ¾ mile.

Parking: In the pub's spacious car park; alternatively in a side road branching off Chandlers Lane, just before the lane crosses the nearby M25.

Length of the walk: 4 miles. Map: OS Landranger 166 Luton, Hertford and surrounding area, or 176 West London Area (GR 065983).

Being within easy reach of Watford's Cassiobury Park, Whippendell Wood is a favourite stamping ground for local residents. We share the pleasure by walking through these woods to the Grand Union Canal and the park, where young walkers can sample the play area (and adults the tea garden) before returning to Chandler's Cross.

The Walk
From the Clarendon Arms go forward into Fir Tree Hill and turn right very soon into Rousebarn Lane. Stay with this tree-shaded lane for ⅓ mile to Blacketts Nursery, a traditional country nursery and well worth a visit. Turn left into a woodland path just beyond the nursery and branch right at a fork after a few yards (110°). This level branch is for humans, the other is for horses. Ignore another horses' branch on the right very soon, and all other branches, and keep forward through the wood.

You will pass two clearings on the right in sequence and separated by an upward slope in the path. The second clearing is identified by a nature trail marker (3) and, after a short distance, by a two-way fork in the path. Take the right-hand branch at the fork (100°), the greenest, more open of the two, and follow this alongside an extensive stand of mature silver birch trees.

After 200 yards you will be joined by a well-used path coming in from the right (over your right shoulder). Go forward with this and stay in the main path when, after 50 yards, you come to a two-way fork. The main path soon bears slightly right and arrives at a small clearing after a further 100 yards, where there is another nature trail

15

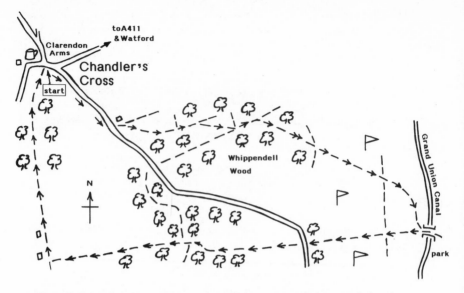

marker (15) and a crossing path. Continue straight on from here, steeply uphill to a magnificent avenue of lime trees.

Walk straight on through the avenue to its far end, in the process crossing a clearing (for golf) and a rough drive – the latter with a notice 'Private Road not open to the Public' misleadingly placed. Go right with the path from the far end of the avenue and you soon find yourself beside the Grand Union Canal, Cassiobury Park. Any young members of your party will doubtless agree to cross the canal bridge and make a beeline for the play area and miniature steam railway in the park, while others may be more interested in the tea garden!

Back at the canal (on the opposite side from the park) climb the short steep slope under trees in line with the canal bridge. This places you at the start of a gradually ascending ½ mile path which takes you straight on – partly under trees, partly over golf course greens. It culminates in a steep descent to Rousebarn Lane opposite a cultivated field. Maintaining the same direction (260°), cross the field to an outcrop of tall trees. When adjacent to the trees go over a stile and forward into another field; then follow the wavering field edge all the way to the far left-hand corner, where you will find no fewer than four stiles. The stiles on the left and right lead into areas managed by the Woodland Trust, a society dedicated to the conservation and main-tenance of trees and woodland, especially ancient woodland.

You should go over the stile directly ahead and into a ½ mile path running straight on between trees on the left and a hedge and field on the right. The path terminates at a stile (to the left of a barn) and forms

16

a T-junction with a track. Turn right here and, after passing a school and an attractive timber-frame cottage follow what soon becomes a path leading into Harrocks Wood – another Woodland Trust property. In due course this straight path (you should ignore all branches) emerges from the wood and runs downhill between paddocks, joining the road at Chandler's Cross.

Commonwood
The Cart and Horses

Situated in a delightful, quiet country corner, the Cart and Horses is understandably popular with walkers, especially those with a healthy appetite or a demanding thirst. The regular food menu is very extensive indeed, and includes starters, snacks (sausages, burgers, sandwiches, for example), jacket potatoes and ploughman's. Fish, chicken and steaks come in a variety of permutations under the main meals heading, and vegetarians are well catered for. If you are game for a challenge (and can give 24 hours notice) you could take on the Ultimate – a gastronomic extravaganza which, along with an 18 ounce T-bone steak, includes 54 ounces of meat. But you had best forget about the walk!

Other than on Sunday, there is no need to plan your visit very precisely as you can eat here at any time between 11 am and 9.30 pm Monday to Saturday (Sunday 12 noon to 2.30 pm and 7 pm to 9.30 pm). Drinking hours are the maximum possible: 11 am to 11 pm Monday to Saturday and 12 noon to 3 pm and 7 pm to 10.30 pm Sunday. So there is rarely a time you cannot stop here for a glass of real ale – Greene King IPA, Marston's Pedigree, Draught Bass or Tolly Original. Cider drinkers should be equally happy with Addlestone's or Red Rock.

Well-behaved dogs are welcome inside, but children under 14 can only be taken into the garden, which has swings, a climbing frame and a climbing tree. On colder days you can stay in this most comfortable of pubs and enjoy the sight and warmth of a real log fire. Telephone: 01923 263763.

How to get there: The pub is in Quickmoor Lane midway between Chipperfield and Sarratt. Approach from Red Lion Lane, Sarratt, or from Bucks Hill via Quickmoor Lane.

Parking: In the pub's own car park or in the lanes nearby.

Length of the walk: 4 miles. Map: OS Landranger 166 Luton, Hertford and surrounding area (GR 047005). Chiltern Society Footpath Map No 5.

You could call this the 'Three Commons Walk' since it includes the commons at Chipperfield, Sarratt and Commonwood. Chipperfield with its church, its cricket pitch and its three pubs is clearly the most popular, especially at weekends when play is in hand. By taking advantage of a short-cut (missing out Sarratt), you can reduce the distance walked from four miles to three.

The Walk
From the pub's car park go along the 'no through road' signposted to Penman's Green. When this road soon turns left go forward through a kissing-gate along a path signposted to King's Langley. This crosses the fields between wire fences (350°) before following a hedge and terminating at a stile by the woodland of Chipperfield Common. Just ahead of you is one of Chipperfield's best-known attractions, the Apostles Pond. Count the number of old lime trees stationed around its bank and after adding the two that are missing you will know why the pond is so named.

Pass to the right of the pond and go forward a few yards to where the main path divides. Take the 'straight on' path, the one with a mound about 100 yards distant (330°). This is a prehistoric burial mound – not a raised platform for archery practice, as I was once told! Veering slightly left from the mound along the wide path between the trees, you will soon have a glimpse of Chipperfield's green. You will also be following a series of waymark posts and passing to the right of one of Chipperfield's venerable sweet chestnut trees. There are about eight of these magnificent specimens in the woods here, each one aged between 400 and 800 years.

After passing post No 1 you will emerge on to the green. You should now aim for the war memorial and then pass to the right of the Two

19

Brewers along The Street. This will take you to the little post office and downhill to a crossing by the Royal Oak. Turn left at the crossing into Dunny Lane and go along this to a stile on the left opposite the last of a line of houses. Moving away from the left-hand hedge, climb the field to a stile at the top and join a narrow path between gardens. At the road ahead you could turn right for the Windmill pub or left for the teashop.

To continue on the walk you should cross the road and take your cue from the rightmost finger of the three-way signpost opposite (170°). This maintains your previous direction and takes you along the left side of a stand of gorse bushes. Stay with the path as it veers briefly right behind the gorse (there is a seat here) to a waymark post (No 13). Then continue in the same direction as before (170°) through the wood, ignoring all crossings until you reach a wide bridleway running along the southern border of the wood.

All being well you should also come face to face with The Folly, a cottage beside the bridleway. Turn left into the bridleway and go along this for 80 yards, where you will be confronted by a wooden gate ahead. Turn right here to a stile and metal gate. This will place you on a wide path with trees left and a field right. When you meet a crossing of ways go forward along the road signposted 'Private road to Hillmeads Farm' (in fact a public right of way) with Hillmeads Farm Cottage immediately on the right.

Passing between the farm buildings go over a stile on the left before reaching the farmhouse, then turn right straight away and resume your former direction. There is another stile very soon which places you along the left edge of a field. Stay with the field edge as it curves left from a cattle trough (160° and ignoring a waymarked path going off to the right) and cross a stile in the far left-hand corner of the field. You will be overlooking an attractive valley as you continue forward and downhill (160°) to the lowest point of the sloping field, where there is a stile, to the left of Dellfield House, which will lead you forward to a rough drive. For a speedy return to the pub (saving one mile) you could bear left from the drive into a path running above Plough Lane, then turn left in the road when you come to a small car park and keep straight on to the pub. For the complete walk turn right in the lane and very soon left over a stile; then uphill in a field along its right-hand edge. After crossing a stile in the field's far right-hand corner you will soon join a tarmac drive which in turn joins the road at Sarratt.

Turn left in the road and follow this up to the top of Sarratt Green by the Boot public house. Then turn left into a narrow path just beyond the pub and soon cross a stile leading into a field.

From here the path curves right towards the field's furthest corner

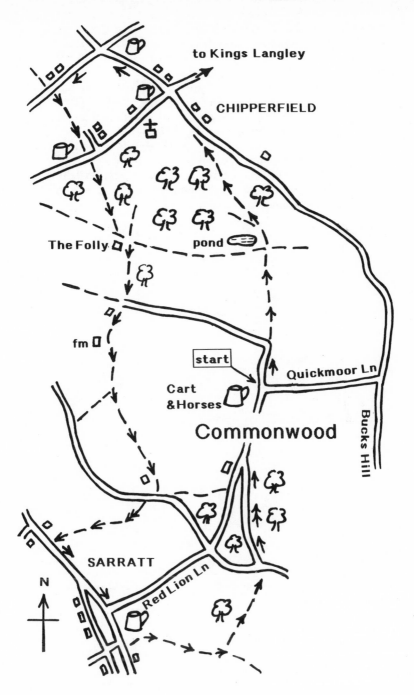

to Kings Langley

CHIPPERFIELD

The Folly

pond

fm

start

Cart
&Horses

Quickmoor Ln

Commonwood

Bucks Hill

SARRATT

N

Red Lion Ln

21

(approx 100°), where three other fields abut. Go forward into the field ahead, aiming for a stile at the centre of its far end (100° from the previous stile) to the left of a tennis court.

Once there turn left so that the tennis court is behind you, and proceed between a wire fence and a hedge of sorts. From the end of this short path continue forward near the left-hand edge of a field. Tall trees and deep pits over to the left make an impressive sight as you cross a stile and go downhill along the right-hand edge of the next field. Turn left in the lane at the bottom (Bottom Lane) and soon right at a T-junction; then climb the hill to another road junction near Commonwood House. By continuing forward you will soon be back at the Cart and Horses.

4 Aldenham
The Round Bush

Technically within the bounds of Aldenham, this pub is in reality in the hamlet with which it shares its name – Round Bush. Having the feel of a true 'local' the pub is obviously very much liked by locals as well as by casual visitors, doubtless on account of its lively but traditional country atmosphere, its good food and its good drink – which includes Benskins, Burton's and Tetley real ales. The pub is open all day 11 am to 11 pm, Mondays to Saturdays, but keeps normal hours on Sunday.

For choice and price the extensive menu will please just about everyone. It ranges from freshly-made 'sarnies', ploughman's and jacket potatoes at one end of the spectrum, to appetising main meals at the other. And anyone with a healthy capacity can round off the meal with one of the delicious sweets – toffee apple tart or chocolate fudge cake, for example. The full menu is available every day lunchtimes and evenings.

Children under 14 can only be taken into the garden, part of which is covered. Dogs are welcome inside but not when food is being served.

Telephone: 01923 857165.

How to get there: The pub is a short distance from the B462 1½ miles south-west of Radlett and one mile from the Junction Five public house on the A41. It is on the opposite side (south) of the B462 from Aldenham village, in the hamlet of Round Bush. Look for the sign to Aldenham Nursery (*not* Summerhouse Lane nearby). Bus 311 from Watford Junction Station stops at Round Bush hourly Monday to Saturday, two-hourly (after 11 am) Sunday. There is a frequent rail service to Watford Junction from London (Euston).

Parking: In the pub's own car park or along the roadside nearby.

Length of the walk: 4¼ miles. Map: OS Landranger 166 Luton, Hertford and surrounding area (GR 145985).

The objective and chief delight of this walk is the river Colne: so near to civilisation with its roads, runways and estates, yet so much apart. This isolation is also enjoyed by Aldenham village near the start of the walk, by Munden House at the turning point and, to a lesser extent, by the well-known Blackbird Farm towards the end.

The Walk

Go right in the road from the Round Bush and soon left in the B462, crossing this to a sidewalk for safety. You will pass the grounds of Edge Grove School before meeting Church Lane on the right. Cross Church Lane to the path opposite and, maintaining the same direction, go along this between trees to Aldenham's churchyard. After following an old brick wall to its corner keep forward through the churchyard, passing to the left of the church and joining the road in Aldenham village.

You should turn right in the road here, but before you do that turn left instead and have a look at the magnificent barns of Church Farm just around the corner. At one time there were plans to convert these barns into residential units and a teashop.

Retracing your steps along the road and passing to the left of the church turn left into the drive signposted to Bricket Wood and Watford Campus. When the drive goes off to the right on its way to the campus, continue forward from a stile and gate along a wide track that runs between trees (hiding a golf course) and fields. Now you must be careful to go through a gap on the left after ¼ mile. This is waymarked with the number 16 and stands near a group of tall Scots pine trees. If you are busy chatting and miss the turning, all is not lost: simply refer to the sketch map and make your way to the first crossing of the river Colne – and skip the next paragraph.

Follow path 16 more or less straight on under the trees (300°) crossing a number of golf course linking paths in the process. When

24

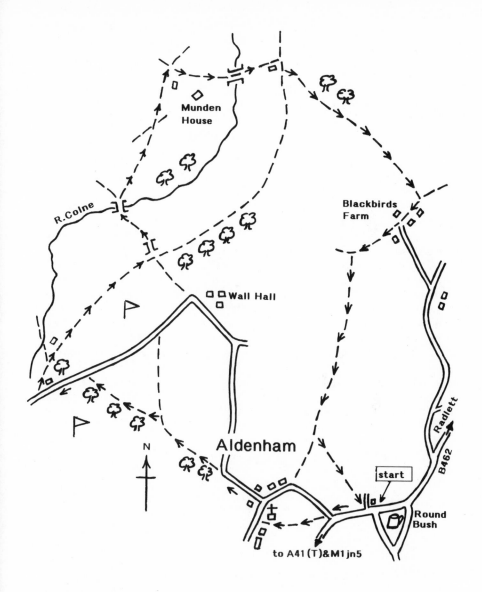

you eventually meet a tarmac drive turn left and go downhill to Otterspool Lodge. Take a hairpin right turn around the lodge and follow a level path parallel to the river Colne. Passing by an iron gate early on (and in view of a thoughtfully designed pumpng station), stay in the path for almost ½ mile to the first crossing. Prior to the crossing you will have noticed the Gothic Wall Hall College, now part of the University of Hertfordshire.

Turn left at the crossing to a footbridge waymarked 12; then over the flat river plain to the river itself and another footbridge. From the second bridge go half-right uphill across the grass, following waymarks numbered 4 (20°) until you meet the tarmac drive to Munden House. Cross the drive to a gravel track and follow this straight on to a stile and gate. From here keep to the right-hand border of a triangular green alongside a lodge house (dated 1880) and turn right, soon passing through a gate numbered 62. From the gate go downhill back to the river Colne – where you have the best view yet of Munden House.

The path from the opposite bank of the river will take you along an avenue of lime trees to a gate by River Lodge. Turn right at the T-junction here and soon left into what becomes an uphill meandering track with woodland on the left. You will in due course come within sight (and perhaps smell) of a sewage farm before the track turns right and enters Blackbirds Farm. Immediately after passing two massive metal barns go through a pair of wide gates on the right and circulate anticlockwise around a concrete farmyard to a track on the far side, guided by waymarks numbered 10. Follow the track downhill between a hedge and a fence and cross a stile on the left at the bottom. From the stile go along the left-hand edge of three large fields in succession.

When you are halfway along the third field you should go over a stile on the left and cross a large meadow half-right (assuming your back is to the stile), passing about 50 yards to the right of a pylon (150°). A stile will take you in the same direction across a school football field to a pedestrian gate adjacent to a school lodge house. This places you on the B462 at Round Bush – close to the Round Bush pub.

Shenley
The Black Lion

⑤

The Black Lion is the first pub you will see as you drive along Shenley's main street from north to south. What you may not immediately notice is its carefully tended garden, where it is a delight to take refreshment on a warm sunny day. When it is not so warm customers can retreat to the small conservatory or into the inner sanctum of the pub itself, where one of the three rooms is suitable for families.

The neatly inscribed blackboard menu is a study in itself, with a vast range of choices from main meals and snacks. The ever-popular ploughman's appears in no less than 15 permutations (more in summer) and there are about 10 sandwich fillings. Vegetarian meals figure prominently, and come with the Vegetarian Society's kite mark. All this every lunchtime and evening, with the option of a roast lunch on Sunday.

Drinking hours are normal, when you can choose from six real ales, one of which is changed fortnightly.

If your dog is a model of good behaviour, he is welcome inside the pub or in the garden.

Telephone: 01923 855728.

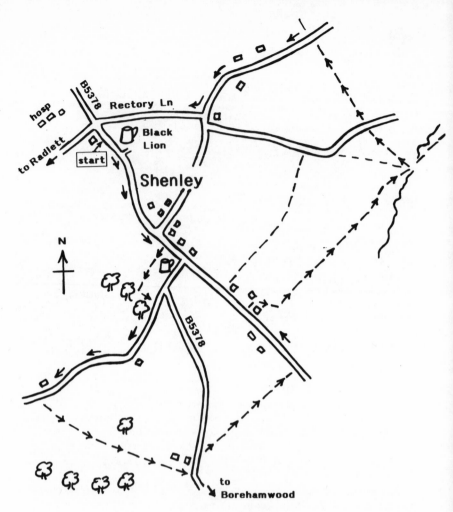

How to get there: The Black Lion is in the main street (London Road) opposite the entrance to Shenley Hospital. It is within easy reach of London Colney (junction 22 of the M25), Borehamwood (along the B5378) and Radlett (along Shenley Hill). Bus 311 from Watford Junction Station and Radlett (near Radlett Station) calls at the Black Lion hourly Monday to Saturday, two-hourly Sunday. Watford Junction connects with London (Euston), Radlett Station with London Thameslink.

Parking: In either of the pub's car parks or along the extensive layby in London Road, but not in front of the school during term time.

28

Length of the walk: 4¼ miles. Map: OS Landranger 166 Luton, Hertford and surrounding area (GR 188008).

Considering the proximity of the M25 motorway, the sense of remoteness along this walk must be experienced to be believed. It crosses a delightful landscape of quiet lanes, fields, woods and undulating hills (hills that are more in view than under foot).

The Walk

When you turn left out of the Black Lion and walk along London Road you will pass the Queen Adelaide pub, the lock up, and the village pond. The lock up was used for the detention of suspected law-breakers prior to their appearance in court. Take note of the two admonishments on this singularly unattractive memorial to the past.

Stay with the main street for ¼ mile and join a footpath on the right (signposted to Woodhall and Radlett Lanes) alongside a garden centre. The path runs between the centre and a hedge before entering woodland at a T-junction. Turn left under the trees and follow the path to a road; then turn right in a delightful no through road and enjoy the scenery. The extensive buildings of Shenley Hospital occupy much of the distant hilltop. The hospital was opened in 1934 and evolved around an existing mansion, Porters Park.

The road will take you into a right-hand curve by Kitwell's Lodge and, after a further ¼ mile, past a pair of attractive semis closely followed by barns. A few yards beyond the barns go over a stile on the left and cross a field half-left (assuming your back is to the road) to another stile in the field's furthest corner (130°), and not necessarily in the direction of the signpost finger.

From that field corner (which could well be temporary) continue in the same direction in the next field, passing close to a single large oak tree and arriving at a gate in a dip and another field. Skimming a woodland edge on your left continue forward (100°) slightly uphill and aiming for a stile ⁴⁄₅ of the way along the right-hand field edge at the far end of woodland. A sighting of rooftops more or less directly ahead should aid you in the navigation. Strike diagonally across the next field to its furthest corner (110°), a little to the right of a large bungalow (another Kitwell's Lodge), and soon join the B5378 road.

Turn left in the road and right after 130 yards into a path signposted to London Road. Walk the right-hand field edge for a few yards only, and enter the scrub on the right, then soon make your exit from the scrub by climbing a stile. You now have a succession of field edges, with hedges on the left, for ⅓ mile to a road. Turn left in the road and go along to Pursley Farm (with its magnificent tiled barn) on the right. There you will find a signpost labelled Mimms Lane directing you through the farmyard. By going half-right between the farm buildings

29

you will meet a farm track on the far side. This soon turns left between the fields, and after a brief foray to the right and forward again, arrives at a gate under a small metal pylon.

It is now a matter of following the left-hand edge of the field gradually downhill into a shallow valley (50°) accompanied by a hedge and a number of fine old oak trees, with which this district is well endowed. If you can see a tall slender aerial mast directly ahead on the skyline, you are likely to be on course. When you eventually cross a built over ditch on entry to another field you should cross that field to its far right-hand corner (50°) – where you should also find a stile.

Now hold it there! Do not continue forward but stay in the same large field, turning acutely left (310°) and ascending the gentle slope along the right-hand of two paths to a stile and a lane, cutting off a large right-hand corner of the field in the process. If you aim for the metal footpath signpost in the upper edge of this field you cannot go far wrong.

Having arrived at the stile you could shorten the walk by ⅓ mile by turning left in this very pleasant lane. Turn right when it terminates, then first left into Rectory Lane. The pub is at the far end of Rectory Lane.

For the full walk (and an opportunity to view some fine houses) cross the lane to a stile opposite (signposted Rectory Lane) and walk the right-hand edge of the field uphill to a stile opposite a farm drive. Turn left in the lane here (Rectory Lane) and follow it for ⅓ mile to a road junction, passing an unusually attractive stud farm dated 1903, also Manor Cottage (some cottage!) and the elegant Shenley Hill, the last house on the left. Keep right at the road junction and, passing Arden Cottage, follow what is still Rectory Lane all the way to the Black Lion.

Colney Heath
The Crooked Billet

6

The licensee of the Crooked Billet looks on his pub as a traditional ale house. It certainly is that, but it is also a pub with a very friendly feel about it, and where good homely food is prepared. There are some excellent baguettes with a choice of fillings, ploughman's with ham, turkey or cheese, and filled jacket potatoes. There is also a good choice of daily specials, such as chilli, tagliatelle and scampi. Food is available every lunchtime. If the weather is suitable a barbecue is fired up on Sundays at lunchtime and all day on bank holiday Mondays.

The traditional ales already alluded to include Theakston Best and Greene King Abbot Ale. Draught cider is Blackthorn Dry. The pub is open for drinking all day Saturday (11 am to 11 pm) throughout the year. On other days the hours are normal. Children under 14 cannot be taken inside, but they will enjoy the garden, with its adventure play area. Dogs are tolerated, but not where food is being served.

Telephone: 01727 822128.

31

How to get there: The pub is situated in Colney Heath's High Street, the village being clearly signposted from the A414 midway between Hatfield and the London Colney turn-off. Bus 342 calls at the Crooked Billet and runs hourly Monday to Saturday (only) from St Albans City Station, where there are frequent connections with London on the Thameslink rail service.

Parking: In the pub's own car park. Roadside parking is not easy.

Length of the walk: 4½ miles. Map: OS Landranger 166 Luton, Hertford and surrounding area (GR 202060).

Years of gravel extraction between Colney Heath and Broad Colney has left a marvellous heritage of inland lakes – a great place for birds and bird-watchers. In addition to crossing Colney Heath this walk circulates around some of these lakes. At the halfway point there is an opportunity to visit Bowmans Farm for its adventure play area and pet's corner (a charge is made for these), and its farm shop and refectory.

The Walk
On leaving the pub turn right and go along the High Street to the first turning on the left, Park Lane. Go forward across the grass from the far end of this no through road and head towards a white bollard beside the river Colne. Turn left over the concrete bridge here and follow the drive towards a group of semi-detached houses. On reaching the houses turn sharp left through a waymarked gap leading on to Colney Heath (80°).

By walking just outside the trees and scrub on the right you will soon meet a waymark post in a wide gap. Keep right along a path under trees, and following closely the fence and field edge, look for a stile on the right after 150 yards. Go into the field here, leaving the trees behind and following a wire fence to a stile and footbridge (220°).

From the footbridge continue straight on along a track across fields, eventually (½ mile) going left with it and into the yard of Tyttenhanger Farm. Having passed through the farm to its entrance on the far side turn very sharp right (under high-voltage wires) into a concrete drive. When the drive soon bears right continue forward across the grass, and as you pass a farmhouse on the right, go slightly left through an earth cutting. This will take you out to what is labelled as a bridlepath running between flooded gravel workings (310°), with a hedge on the right.

From the end of the bridlepath go through a gate and across the river Colne to a stile. Turn left from the stile and walk between the

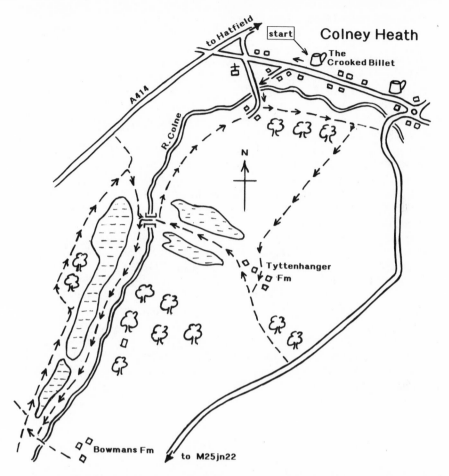

right bank of the Colne and the shore of a ½ mile long lake. The silos of Bowmans Farm will soon come into view, and the façade of Tyttenhanger Park will be seen through the trees on the left. When the lake terminates and is followed by another (they have been known to merge after prolonged rain), a metal gate leads you forward into a farm track that soon runs below the buildings of Bowmans Farm.

Bowmans is more than just a farm: children's play area, tractor rides, shop and refectory are among the things on offer. It is also a valuable resource for school parties who come here to study the complexities of animal husbandry. Before you go dashing off in that direction I should mention that with the exception of the shop and refectory, an entrance charge is levied.

33

When the track curves right near the end of the second lake, go through a metal gate in a corner and turn right on a farm track. Turn right again quite soon (after crossing a ditch) and keep forward through a gap, ignoring a concrete drive going half-left, uphill. The lakes will still be on your right as you double back and walk this level track for ⅓ mile.

Stay on the track when it turns half-left (at the end of that ⅓ mile), and likewise when it resumes its previous direction, walking alongside a wood and passing to the left of a pylon. (Your OS map may show the path passing to the right of the wood and crossing the water, which is fine if you have come prepared for a swim!)

Go through a gate on the right leading to a small parking area and continue forward again, with a hedge soon on the left and the water down to the right. Ignoring a branch heading off to a stile and gate on the left, circulate clockwise around the head of the lake (almost doubling back) and aim for a fenced enclosure about 200 yards ahead, which you will remember from earlier in the walk.

Turn left through the enclosure (using the stile) and cross the river Colne, then turn left and follow the river bank, doubling back yet again. Your path soon leaves the river and passes to the right of trees. It crosses a quarry drive and continues forward between a hedge and (later) a high bank (60°), and in due course evolves into a gravel drive.

When you pass the waterworks and find yourself among houses you will know that this is where you came in and that you will soon need to go left with the drive to the river bridge. Having crossed the bridge turn right immediately and make your way across the grass to Park Lane, and along this to Colney Heath High Street and the Crooked Billet.

7 Bedmond
The Bell

Bedmond can be justly proud of its history: it was the birthplace of Nicholas Breakspear, the only English Pope (1154–1159). It can also be proud of its present, in having such a welcoming local in its midst. This is certainly the place to be if you have a hearty appetite and can pack away sizeable meals – although it might be wise to reserve the pleasure until after the walk.

There is a wide choice – from the snack menu (jacket potatoes, sandwiches, ploughman's and so on), the main hot menu or the specials board. Unfortunately, this good food can only be enjoyed Monday to Saturday lunchtime. However, if you are buying drinks the licensee is happy for you to eat your own food in the garden when meals are not available. But if you are leading a walking party, do please ask about this beforehand, as it is only a small garden. If you simply cannot survive without that hot Sunday lunch or bar meal, I suggest that you eat at The Swan, Pimlico, about 3 miles into the walk.

There are usually three real ales: Tetley Bitter, Greene King IPA and Burton Ale. Drinking hours are normal. Dogs are welcome inside if kept well at heel, but children under 14 can only be taken into the garden.

Telephone: 01923 262910.

How to get there: The Bell is in Bedmond's main street within easy reach of Hemel Hempstead (near junction 8 of the M1) and Kings Langley (near junction 20 of the M25). From Kings Langley join Church Lane (opposite the Rose and Crown) followed by Water Lane and (under the railway) Tom's Lane, turning right at Bedmond's roundabout. Bus 344 from Watford Junction Station runs half-hourly Monday to Saturday, hourly Sunday. There is a frequent train service from London (Euston) to Watford Junction.

Parking: In one of the Bell's two car parks, or in Tom's Lane off the nearby roundabout.

Length of the walk: 5 miles. Map: OS Landranger 166 Luton, Hertford and surrounding area (GR 099035).

This walk crosses a surprisingly rural piece of countryside in an otherwise densely populated part of Hertfordshire. There are some good views, both local and distant; but since part of the walk is shared with our four-footed friends, there is likely to be some mud.

The Walk
On leaving the Bell go right and over the roundabout to a footpath on the left signposted 'Hemel Hempstead and Kings Langley'. This is opposite a corrugated-iron church (the only one of its kind with a spire, apparently) on the corner of Serge Hill Lane. The path runs alongside a housing estate and after 200 yards you are in a field. Cross the middle of the field straight on towards the right-hand end of a small group of trees. Once there turn half right in the next field (280°), roughly in line with a distant barn and aiming for a stile and another field.

Maintaining the same direction, cross this much larger field to a waymarked cattle trough at its centre and continue straight on to a stile at a lane. As you cross the field you may hear the occasional Euston line train running along the Gade Valley one mile to the west. Turn left in the lane and right over a stile after 25 yards. From here follow a field's right-hand edge to another lane. Turn left in this second lane and stay with it for a short distance until it completes an S bend, then leave it for a field on the right at a stile.

Cross the field diagonally (300°, half-left) to a pair of stiles in its furthest corner, while taking note of the old farmhouse (Hyde Farm) over to your left as you proceed. From the second stile (the one beside a metal gate) turn left in a track and pass between barns in a farmyard to a three-way waymark post, where there's another sighting of the farmhouse. Turn right at the post (for Bunkers Lane) and follow the

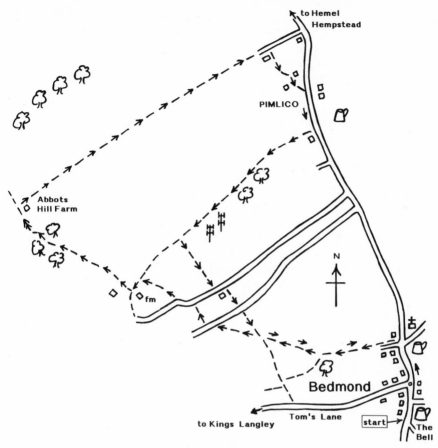

left-hand edge of a field (320°) alongside the grounds of Pimlico House.

When the grounds terminate after 200 yards look for a gap on the left where two steps will take you into a path under trees. Go downhill in the path, with a field and wire fence left, to a stile at the bottom. Keep straight on from the stile, climbing the opposite slope along the left edge of a rough pasture (290°), while not omitting to look back at the view.

A house (Abbots Hill Farm) comes into view as you follow the left curve of the field edge to a stile and into a footpath under trees (resuming your previous direction); after which you will pass the left side of the house to its drive. By crossing the drive to a narrow waymarked track opposite you will be at the start of a straight one mile bridleway. This is accompanied by a hedge on the right and will take

37

you as far as Highwood Hall where the bridleway becomes a tarmac drive. You could now either go along the drive to Pimlico, then turn right and walk the busy road for ¼ mile to the Swan pub (and skip the next paragraph), or opt for a short but complicated country route to the same point by turning right at a gate just beyond Highwood Hall.

For the country route you must squeeze past the gate (note the footpath sign opposite the gate) and pass to the right of a barn to a stile, then along the right-hand edge of a meadow and in a narrow path between hedges to another meadow. Cross this meadow half-left to a metal gate and then turn left and almost immediately right through a riding school. This will take you to a field gate on the left side of a house. Cross the field half-left to a stile and turn right in the road there.

Join a footpath on the right 50 yards after passing the Swan pub (which is where you can get that Sunday lunch) and just prior to cottage No 3. This path runs between gardens left and a riding school right (which may explain that earlier muddy bridleway) and soon between fields, with a hedge left. Woodland takes over from the hedge, and when this terminates two stiles lead you forward along the left edge of another field. When you have passed the second of two aerial masts by one left-hand field length (about 150 yards) you should turn left into this field and follow what to you will be its right-hand edge. When you reach the field's far right-hand corner a narrow path will take you forward (along with the overhead wires) to a lane. Turn left in the lane and, after passing Hyde Lane Farm, right to a stile and gate signposted 'Tom's Lane ½'. Then follow a right-hand hedge to a stile and another lane.

Cross the lane to a signposted gap leading into a very large field. Strike across the field (150°) to a cattle trough at its centre (which I'm sure you will remember), then turn half-left from the trough (110°) and straight on in the next field, heading for the left-hand end of a line of trees. As you pass the trees bear slightly left across the next (the final) field and soon find yourself alongside a housing estate and back in Bedmond, where you should turn right for the Bell.

8 Berkhamsted
The Boat

A feast of colourful flowers awaits today's 'boat people' cruising past this canalside pub on a summer's day. Were they to tie up, they could also enjoy a culinary feast, in more than ample proportions and at prices to suit the leanest of pockets. The main meals come as five or six specials chalked on the blackboard, while the old favourites (the sandwiches, ploughman's, omelettes, salads and so on) appear on a regular menu card. Children's portions are available on request, but if under 14 the children can only be taken on to the patio. As it overlooks the canal, this is an interesting place for them to be.

The quality of the food is in part attributed to three excellent local suppliers: butcher, fishmonger and baker. The butcher is just across the road and is worth a visit, if only to view. Meals are served Monday to Saturday lunchtimes, and Monday evening. The barbecue is in action every Sunday lunchtime during the summer – outside if it is dry, inside if wet. Dogs are not welcome inside when food is being served.

Drinking hours are normal; real ales are Fuller's Chiswick Bitter, London Pride, ESB and (in winter only) Mr Harry. There is also a wide selection of wines by the glass.

Telephone: 01442 877152.

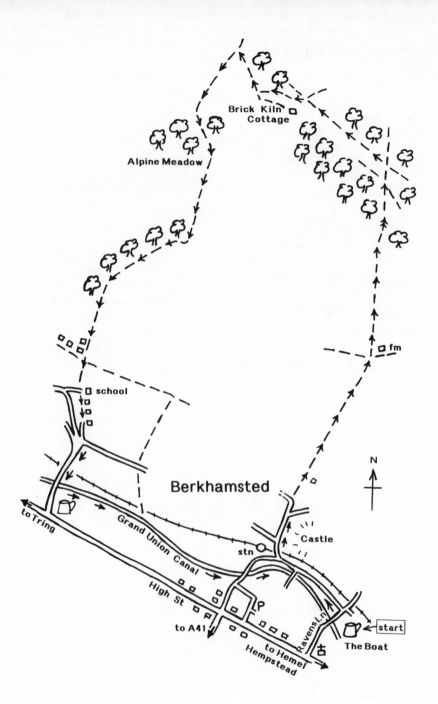

Brick Kiln Cottage

Alpine Meadow

fm

school

Berkhamsted

to Tring

Grand Union Canal

stn

Castle

N

High St

to A41

Ravens Ln

to Hemel Hempstead

start

The Boat

How to get there: The Boat stands beside the canal bridge where Ravens Lane runs into Gravel Path (a road). You can join Ravens Lane from the Baptist church in Berkhamsted High Street. There is a frequent rail service from London (Euston) Monday to Saturday. On Sunday the service is hourly. The station is ⅓ mile from the Boat. Leave the station from the booking hall side and go left along Lower Kings Road towards the Crystal Palace pub; then along the canal towpath to the Boat.

Parking: The pub has only a small car park. Roadside parking is possible but limited. Alternative parking is available opposite the castle in Castle Hill.

Length of the walk: 5¼ miles. Map: OS Landranger 165 Aylesbury and Leighton Buzzard (GR 997078).

Almost from the start this walk makes a beeline for the heights of Berkhamsted Common. Once there, it enjoys a tantalising mile of heath and open woodland of birch, oak and bracken. Back in Berkhamsted the walk concludes with one mile of the Grand Union Canal towpath.

The Walk

Cross the road from the Boat and go along the canal towpath (canal on your left) as far as the Crystal Palace pub. Join the road here and continue forward towards the railway station. Just prior to the station go under the railway bridge and along Brownlow Road with Berkhamsted Castle ruins on your right. When Brownlow Road curves right go forward into Castle Hill, and when this turns left, over a stile adjacent to the cricket club drives.

The right-hand drive will take you up to one of the club's car park, from which point you should continue forward but now on grass and roughly following a line of electricity wires in the dip of the fields with a hedge on your left. You will cross a succession of stiles before passing to the left of farm buildings. Continue forward in the dip, but now along a track and with a hedge on your right. When the dip curves left beyond a stile, keep straight on uphill to a stile and into a wood.

The path climbs steeply through the wood, curving slightly left in an area of silver birch trees and meeting a junction of five ways when it is almost at its highest point. Continue forward from the junction, in open woodland along a wide grassy track, and join another junction (six or seven ways this time) after only 80 yards. Take the second exit on the left (320° and running parallel with the first) and follow this wide bridleway straight on through the wood for almost ½ mile.

At the end of the ½ mile you will meet a junction of ways centred on a large patch of gravel, with Brick Kiln Cottage and its drive over to your left and an extensive meadow on your right. Branch half-left here (260°) and, passing a private garden gate, follow the meandering path through the trees for a few hundred yards to a private field gate, ignoring a branch on the right as you go. Turn right at the T-junction by the field gate (340°) and walk under the trees parallel to the long field edge until you come to a stile on the left leading into that same field. Go over the stile and follow a succession of two right-hand field edges (220°) to a stile at the entrance to Alpine Meadow, a nature reserve on land leased by the Herts and Middlesex Wildlife Trust. The sloping chalk grassland is the main interest here for its wealth of wildflowers and insects.

Go downhill into the dip of the reserve (170°), then straight on up to a stile and out into a field. Turn right and climb steeply with trees on the right to a stile and gate leading into another field. Straight on now, with a hedge on the right, all the way to a woodland corner, with Berkhamsted's old water tower in view 1½ miles ahead. Turn right at the corner and follow the long line of trees (260°) as it gradually curves left.

You will pass a small pond on the left and a couple of bungalows on the right before reaching a stile in the field's far right-hand corner. Forward now over a crossing and into a path that passes Bridgewater School. Keep to the tarmac path that soon branches left behind gardens and, when it turns left to pass between houses, continue forward in an unsurfaced path. When the path runs into a drive, follow this straight on down to a road junction. Cross Bridgewater Road (to the left of the junction) and continue downhill over the railway and the canal. Double back to join the canal towpath (effectively turning left from the road) and follow the canal for 1 mile into the heart of Berkhamsted.

The railway station (and Castle Hill where you may have left your car) can be accessed via the first (iron) road bridge after ¾ mile of towpath. To finish at the Boat continue to the next road bridge and cross this to the opposite bank (near the Crystal Palace pub) then go along the next stretch of towpath back to the Boat.

Wilstone
The Half Moon

The Half Moon is an attractive well-kept village pub with a number of very definite pluses, including a no smoking dining-room where children may be taken and, equally important, a warm welcome for walkers. In the winter months you can enjoy the warmth and welcoming sight of a real log fire, and in the summer the large garden – where there is a play area for children.

Top of the bill for eating is the steak and kidney pie made to the licensee's own recipe, and (she modestly admits) by her own hand. She is also well pleased with the specially cured Farmhouse Ham. Her Scottish husband is doubtless responsible for the haggis, a true taste of Scotland sent down from Lockerbie. These, among a score of appetising choices, make up a very reasonably priced menu, to say nothing of the ploughman's, jacket potatoes, burgers, sandwiches and the childrens' menu. Monday is the one day in seven that food is not served, but you can drink on any day at normal hours. There is a choice of at least three real ales: Bass, Flowers Original and a guest beer. Draught cider is Blackthorn Dry. Dogs may be brought inside if kept on a lead.

Telephone: 01442 826410.

How to get there: From the A41 at Aston Clinton (by the Rising Sun pub and 2½ miles west of Tring), take the B489 signposted to Ivinghoe. Turn left for Wilstone after 1½ miles.

Parking: In the pub's own car park or along the roadside nearby.

Length of the walk: 4¾ miles. Map: OS Landranger 165 Aylesbury and Leighton Buzzard (GR 905141).

Your enjoyment of this walk may well arise from the tranquillity and quietness that is everywhere along its route – as you tread the towpath of the Aylesbury Canal, view the ruined church of Long Marston and cross level fields on your return to Wilstone.

The Walk
Turn right on leaving the Half Moon and go along to the village hall. Go right with the road there, then left into a rough drive after a few yards. You will pass a small playground on the left and house number 53 on the right, and soon arrive at the canal. You now have 1½ miles of this peaceful canal, peaceful because it only flows from Marsworth on the Grand Union Canal to Aylesbury, a distance of about six miles. The original plan to link this branch to the Oxford Canal at Abingdon came to nothing, and it has seen little traffic since the end of the 19th century. In 1964 plans were afoot to close it altogether. The Aylesbury Canal Society came to the rescue and its future is now secure.

Walking left along the towpath you will soon go under two bridges – each carrying footpaths, and a road bridge after ¾ mile. The road bridge is accompanied by a lock cottage. Stay on the towpath for about ½ mile to the next bridge (numbered 8). Cross the bridge and go along the lane, soon turning left with it by Canal Farm. Immediately after the turn, go over a stile on the right and along a path behind farm buildings. Turn left from the next stile and enter the left-hand field; then turn right and, resuming your previous direction, follow a succession of two right-hand field edges. Turn left out of the furthest field corner and walk parallel to a hedge and ditch, soon meeting a stile and a farm drive. Turn right onto the drive and follow this to the road by Shirley Cottage, Puttenham. Go straight on through the village, turning left into a no through road beyond Grange Farm. This leads to St Mary's church with its interesting chequerboard tower of flint and chalk.

Climb a stile to the right of the churchyard gate and cross a field (60°) to a pair of stiles on opposite banks of a ditch. Walk straight on in the next field for 50 yards to a gated footbridge on the left, and once

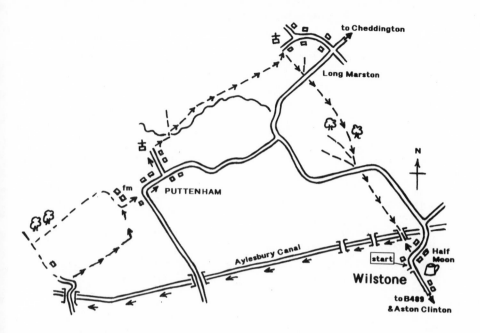

over this turn right immediately (not obeying the waymark) and make for a stile and gate placed centrally at the end of the field. The stile will take you into a very large field, where you should aim for the distant church tower at Long Marston, while keeping parallel to the tree-lined brook on the right (60°).

When the brook eventually curves off to the right (taking the field edge with it) you should continue forward aiming to the right of the church (70°) and to a stile in the field's far right-hand corner. If you arrive at the corner of an L-shaped brook under an electricity pole with wires branching three ways, you are in the right place. Continue forward again to a stile in the next field's far right-hand corner, and to another stile almost immediately. From the stile go half-left across a small field to a road by Long Marston's ruined church. The church (only the tower remains) dates back to the 15th century and was demolished around 1880.

To continue on the walk re-enter that small field (almost doubling back) from a footpath signpost near Old Church Cottage. This directs you across the field to a footbridge, which in turn places you in a larger field. Cross this straight on (in line with the footbridge) to a stile on the far side (140°), at a road. As you walk that field you may notice the deep furrows which are reminders of early ploughing methods.

45

Cross the road to the footpath signposted 'Wilstone 1' and follow this between hedges to a stile and along the left-hand edge of a field, then forward across what appears to have once been a tiny field to a stile and ditch, and straight on again to a pair of stiles and a ditch in the far right-hand corner of a field. In the next field you should go forward a short distance (30 yards) to a stile on the right leading into scrubby trees. I hope you are still with me in this complexity of stiles and ditches.

After pursuing the twisting path through the scrub to a footbridge you will emerge into an open grassy area, better described as a piece of no man's land. Keep more or less straight on through this (160°), with taller trees in view ahead and a field on the right, until you reach a quiet lane. Cross the lane to a gate and a stile and go straight on parallel to the left-hand edge of a field (160°). When the field divides into two parts separated by a thin line of trees, go into the left-hand part, and forward to the stile at the far end. Cross the stile into the corner of a sharply angled field, and, cutting off that corner, soon enter the next field. All that remains is to cross this final field to a footbridge over the canal (140°). Wilstone is straight on.

Flamstead
The Three Blackbirds

The Three Blackbirds stands in a prominent position at the centre of Flamstead, and is one of many attractive buildings in the village. Part of it dates back 400 to 500 years, predating the lovely terrace of almshouses which faces it across the High Street. The pub is equally attractive inside, and maintains a comfortable atmosphere in which to eat and drink.

The Les Routiers certificate which graces the bar is an acknowledgement of the 'warm welcome' and 'quality and value good food' obtainable here. Only a few words, but they speak volumes. Hertfordshire's pubs often specialise in home-made steak and ale pie, but here it is different – steak and mushroom! If this does not take your fancy there is an extensive regular menu to choose from. This should satisfy just about everyone – including the children, who are very welcome here.

The real ale enthusiast should also feel happy here, with four brews at his disposal – Webster's Yorkshire, Ruddles County, Directors and a guest beer. Meals are served every lunchtime and evening except Sunday evening, and drinking hours are normal. Your dog is welcome (if well behaved) but not in the main dining area.

Telephone: 01582 840330.

How to get there: If travelling north along the A5183/A5 from St Albans turn left into Chequers Hill soon after passing junction 9 of the M1. Flamstead is ½ mile along this road. Bus 343 runs from St Albans City railway station hourly Monday to Saturday, two-hourly on Sunday. Trains run daily at frequent intervals from London to St Albans on the Thameslink rail service.

Parking: In the pub's small car park. If this is full you could look for a place in the High Street or by the chuchyard in Trowley Hill Road.

Length of the walk: 4½ miles. Map: OS Landranger 166 Luton, Hertford and surrounding area (GR 078146).

This walk crosses a peaceful undulating landscape punctuated with large attractive farmhouses and with farms that seem to prosper. There are wide views from quiet tracks and lanes, and woodlands graced with bluebells in springtime. There may also be mud, so do carry a pair of wellies, and a walking stick for stability!

The Walk
From the Three Blackbirds go left into Trowley Hill Road, passing the churchyard and joining a path on the right just after Pound Farm (a farm in name only). This path runs between a hedge and a fence and enters a field at the far end. Turn left there and go downhill behind gardens to the first field corner (there is another, later). From that first corner continue in the same direction, but now between a garden left and a field right. A very fine house (Trowley Hill) comes into view before you arrive at a narrow road.

Turn left in the road and immediately right into White Hill, following this down to Trowley Bottom. Keep straight on past Trowley Bottom Farm and uphill in the lane; then branch right at a Y-junction and keep going uphill. Soon after passing Chalkdell Cottages leave the road by entering the wide concrete drive to Grove Farm on the left. Go forward between the barns (perhaps not under the silo) and soon curve right, passing to the left of the farmhouse (sideways on) and aiming for a fieldside track running uphill beyond the farm.

At the top of the hill the track passes a cow shed (where I saw some of the most handsome cows ever) and eventually forms a T-junction with another track, Green Lane. Turning right in this you may soon – depending on recent weather – be glad you took my advice and carried wellies and a walking stick.

After ¼ mile the track turns right and becomes wider, so that your feet have more choice. After a further ⅓ mile it is met by a lane coming in from the right. There is a pond here, and along the lane to

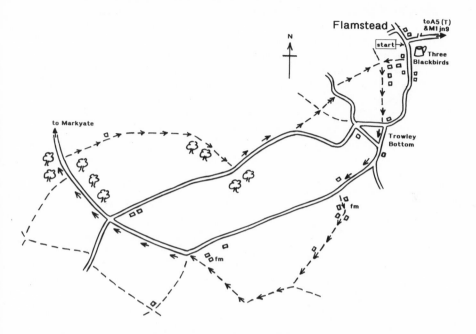

the right Puddephats Farm and its barns, which are well worth a closer look. Go forward in the lane, maintaining your previous direction and enjoying the many varieties of shrubs and trees lining its route.

When you arrive at a crossing continue forward again (Markyate direction) in what is a busier road. And when the wood on the right comes to an abrupt end after ⅓ mile turn right into a rough drive signposted as a footpath. This drive follows the wood edge and leads to an attractive farm cottage. Cross a stile on the right just prior to the cottage and resume your previous direction, but now along a left-hand field edge. Cross another stile in the field's far left-hand corner and continue forward another 30 yards. Ignore a stile on the left at this point and turn half right, crossing a large field diagonally to the near corner of a wood (110°).

Enter the wood from a stile and follow a waymarked path through the trees. When the path eventually emerges from the left side of the wood, turn right and follow the wood-edge; and after the wood terminates keep straight on across the fields to a lane. Turn left in the lane and follow it for ¼ mile or so until it goes into a half-right curve. Go through a gap on the left just before the curve (there is a footpath signpost on the opposite side of the road) and downhill to a crossing in the dip of the fields (40°); then straight on uphill to a stile and a lane.

Turn left in the lane and right into a footpath after 50 yards, crossing a field in the direction of Flamstead's church (70°). This will in due course place you in the same narrow path that marked the start of the walk, at the end of which you should turn left.

Before you jump back into your car (or on to the bus) do take a walk along the High Street and along River Hill opposite the Spotted Dog. The church is also worth a visit for its famous wall paintings; but since you may well find it locked, you will need to be content with a perambulation of the churchyard, where there are graves dating back to the plague of 1604.

Redbourn
11 The Hollybush

The Hollybush is a delightful pub in an incomparable setting amongst well-kept cottages and close to Redbourn's parish church. Once inside you can take pleasure in the pub's traditional atmosphere, helped along by the nicely polished brass and copper, by the open fire, and by the licensee's warm welcome.

The menu card at the Hollybush presents an adequate choice of bar meals at reasonable prices. This is expanded by dishes of the day chalked on the blackboard. Here may be found lasagne, beef and mushroom pie, vegetable goulash and so on. Food is home-cooked and freshly prepared to order, and is available Monday to Saturday lunchtimes only, with a slightly reduced choice on Saturday. If the absence of food at other times is a drawback you could try the Cricketers not far away across Redbourn Common or the Bull in High Street.

Children under 14 cannot be accommodated inside. On a fine day they will be happy enough in the garden, but if it turns to rain they can be taken into the old school room behind the pub.

Real ales include Tetley Bitter, Benskins Best Bitter and a special beer, and draught cider is Scrumpy Jack. All this during normal pub

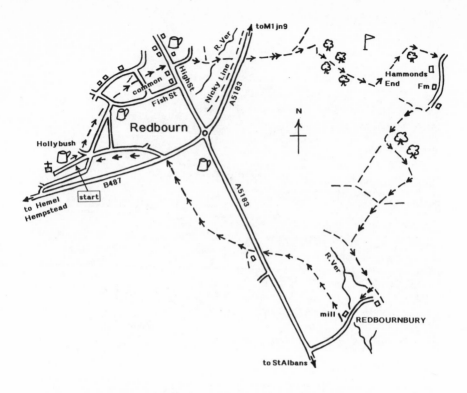

hours. Your dog may keep you company, but not while food is being served.
Telephone: 01582 792423.

How to get there: The pub is near the parish church in Church End, just beyond the south-western extremity of Redbourn Common. Approach from the B487 along Hemel Hempstead Road or Chequer Lane, or from Redbourn's High Street along Fish Street. Bus 307 from Harpenden stops on the common nearby and runs hourly Monday to Saturday only. There is a frequent service daily to Harpenden from London on the Thameslink rail service.

Parking: In the pub's own car park or along the roadside adjacent to Redbourn Common. There is also a small car park on the common, near the cricket club and a short distance along the walk.

Length of the walk: 5 miles. Map: OS Landranger 166 Luton, Hertford and surrounding area (GR 101117).

I owe the idea for this enjoyable walk to the staff of the Countryside Management Service, who conduct parties along its circular route from the restored Redbournbury Mill. Although the central theme is the much talked about river Ver (on which the mill depends) the walk also enjoys the gentle heights around Hammonds End Farm and the fine old buildings of Redbourn.

The mill is open to the public on bank holiday weekends and other selected weekends. Light refreshments are usually available.

The Walk

From the Hollybush go along Church End towards the common and join a tarmac path just beyond Mymms Cottage. The path crosses the common accompanied by an avenue of trees; it passes to the right of the cricket clubhouse and comes in sight of the Brooke Bond tea factory. This factory which is well over to your right, replaced an earlier silk mill. Nothing remains of the mill – except a bell.

The tarmac path crosses Lybury Lane and later divides two ways. Take the right-hand branch (straight on) and follow this over another road and between brick walls to Redbourn's High Street. Looking left along the High Street you will see the Bull public house, an important staging-post in times past. It was one of 18 hostelries that existed here when Redbourn was on a main highway (Watling Street) to the north.

Cross to Waterend Lane opposite and follow it straight on when it changes to a rough drive staying with this when it crosses the river Ver at a ford. After passing a nursery go uphill in a narrow path to the Nicky Line and Redbourn's bypass. The Nicky Line is the trackbed of the former Hemel Hempstead to Harpenden railway. It is managed as a wildlife habitat and is used by walkers and cyclists.

Cross the bypass (with great care) to a flight of steps opposite. From the top of the flight walk slightly left (about 70°) and uphill across a field, following a line of overhead wires. This will take you into another field at the top, at its corner. Ignore the path going half-left across the field and continue forward, following the right-hand hedge (still 70°) until you come face to face with an area of scrub. This is about ⅓ of the way along the field that you are now in. Turn right here with the waymark arrow (180°) then left into the scrub after only 40 yards.

As you make your way along the well-used path through the scrub (150°) your view through the trees is of the Ver valley on one side and a golf course on the other. The path comes out into the open at a corner of the golf course, where there is a water tap for thirsty golfers. Pass to the right of the tap and turn left from the corner, then follow the hedge (60°) until you reach another area of hawthorn scrub, where there is another tap in view half-left. Turning right into the scrub (along with the waymark arrow) you will view a further part of the golf course left and a field right, and very soon the lovely three-storied Hammonds End House.

Stay with the wire fence as it curves right to a stile, and shortly to another stile at a tarmacked farm drive. Turning right in the drive you will pass a preserved pond before going through the farmyard. Follow the drive as it passes a barn and becomes a track. Turn right with it and soon left (ignoring a branch going straight on along a field edge) eventually following a short wood edge (240°) on the left. You should turn left when you reach the corner of the wood (not straight on across the fields) and follow a longer wood edge (the same wood) downhill.

When you get to the bottom, turn right and follow the dip of the fields, with a hedge first left then right. This will take you down to a defunct fenced and gated watercress farm. Go left in the track just here and follow this to a ford and footbridge over the river Ver. The Ver has suffered badly over a number of years, much of it being totally dry due to drought and excessive extraction. Thanks to the concerted efforts of the Ver Valley Society, this part of the river flows again in all its beauty.

Once across the water (a right-hand turn) soon cross another foot-bridge and make your way forward to Redbournbury Mill. Although there was a mill here at the time of the Domesday Book (1086), much of the present building dates from 1790 – except those parts rebuilt after a fire in 1987. This privately owned mill is supported by English Heritage and is open to the public on selected days throughout the year.

Turn right and join a path to the left of the mill (through a gate, not the adjacent track) and shortly cross two stiles leading into a field. Follow the field edge, with a hedge on the right, for ½ mile to the A5183. Cross the road to Dolittle Mill House opposite and, passing to the right of the house, soon (30 yards) cross a stile leading into a field on the right. Stay with the left-hand hedge of the field to a stile in the far left-hand corner; then keep straight on, but now along the right-hand edge of a field, to Redbourn's bypass.

Cross the bypass to Chequer Lane and stay with this as far as the common, then forward into Church End and the Hollybush. With your observant eye you will have noticed, at the entrance to Church End, the oldest house in Redbourn. This is the Jolly Gardeners, complete with gnome. Also, beyond the pub, an inscription on a one-time workhouse.

12 Coleman Green
The John Bunyan

On a quiet country lane and with an outlook across fields and trees, the John Bunyan is a great place to be on a summer's day, and in winter the warm glow of the log fire makes it a welcome retreat from the cold. It goes without saying that the pub is named after the author of *The Pilgrim's Progress*, but more of that as we set off on the walk.

There are no fewer than 10 main meals to choose from, and these can be accompanied by jacket potatoes, chips or an enormous salad. Vegetarians are catered for, as are those who prefer sandwiches, ploughman's or soup. Sweets include apple pie, Cointreau ice-cream and spotted dick. With the beams and walls occupied by 300 or so jugs and plates, you may fail to notice the framed Clean Food Award and Cellar Award certificates. The latter should give you assurance that the real ale – McMullen's Country Best Bitter and Original AK – is well kept. A guest beer is also available.

Meals can be enjoyed every lunchtime and evening except Sunday evening. Drinking hours are normal. Your dog may join you in this two-bar pub, but your children (if under 14) may not. The law being what it is, you must hope for good weather, so that your children can sit in the garden.

Telephone: 01582 832037.

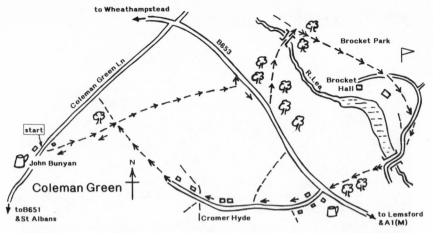

How to get there: Coleman Green is ¾ mile south-east of Wheathampstead as the crow flies, and lies on Coleman Green Lane (mapped as a Roman road). If driving north from St Albans along the B651, branch right into Coleman Green Lane just beyond Sandridge and, keeping left at the first junction, drive straight on for 1½ miles.

Parking: In the pub's own car park or off the lane nearby.

Length of the walk: 4½ miles. Map: OS Landranger 166 Luton, Hertford and surrounding area (GR 190126).

Soon after leaving the John Bunyan this walk launches into a marvellous sunken track and takes you all the way down to Brocket Park in the valley of the river Lea. The park, with its fine hall and lake is a sight to behold, well worth the gentle effort that is then required for the return journey.

The Walk
Go left along the lane from the John Bunyan and soon leave this for a bridleway on the right almost opposite a terrace of tall houses dated 1877. The faded plaque on the sad cottage ruin just here leaves us in no doubt why this remnant has been retained and fenced – and why the John Bunyan pub was so named:

John Bunyan is said by tradition to have preached and occasionally to have lodged in the cottage of which this chimney was a part.

You now have a straight mile of track, mostly hedge-lined and sunken, all the way down to the B653 by Brocket Park. Legally this track is a 'byway open to all traffic'. In practice wheeled traffic might find it

56

difficult, which is fortunate as far as we are concerned. Before the halfway point you will go over a crossing; and when you are in close proximity to the B653 the track (more akin to a path at this point) makes a sharp left-hand turn and goes up to meet the road.

Turn right in the road (cross over for safety) and walk the short distance to a stile on the left – halfway along a parking layby. Here a notice announces Brocket Estate which is crossed by a number of public rights of way.

The well-used path through the trees soon widens and drops down to the river Lea. At a crossing 50 yards beyond the river (there is a private gate directly ahead) a waymark post points to Lemsford. Turn right here and climb the short steep slope under the trees, following the waymark posts to a stile and gate ahead. Continue forward from the stile, in line with the waymarks but now across a golf course.

You will soon be following a wooden fence and enjoying a good view of Brocket Hall and its lake. Built between 1760 and 1780 the hall has been home to two prime ministers – Lord Palmerston and Lord Melbourne. It is now a luxury hotel and conference centre. The park was laid out by 'Capability' Brown. Whether he would have approved of the golf, I am not sure.

An overgrown U-shaped pit and a large gas cyclinder ('Capability' would not have approved) marks the conclusion of that long fence. Here a waymark beckons you half-right into a fenced path, which in turn meets a tarmac drive at a crossing. A right turn in the drive (the right of way is actually on the grass alongside) will take you past the main entrance gate and down to the river bridge, where you have the classic view of Brocket Hall and its lake.

Leave the drive by continuing straight on from the bridge, climbing the waymarked grassy slope (260°) to meet a wood edge at the top. Keeping to the right of the trees stay with them until you are back at the B653. Left from this point is the Crooked Chimney pub, with a name that needs no explanation. Cross to Cromer Hyde Lane, the no through road opposite, and go along this between a number of desirable cottages and forward into open country.

The lane continues for a further ½ mile, with more cottages to delight the eye (especially 12 and 14) and various paths leading from the left and right. When adjacent to a farmhouse and its pond the lane changes to a track and ascends to a high point, giving extensive views across country, including the Lea valley down on the right.

When you have gone straight on over this high point (such as it is) and descended to a dip, you will recognise the sunken path that characterised the start of the walk. All that remains is to turn left in this and make your way back to the John Bunyan.

13 Essendon
The Salisbury Crest

The Salisbury Crest owes much of its popularity to its unique setting in a lovely Hertfordshire village where cottages and cottage gardens vie for attention. So good is the view from the pub's garden that customers are often seen with binoculars and cameras at the ready, or watching the sunsets that its easterly aspect enjoys. When it is too chilly to be out there in the garden, they enjoy sitting in the small but comfortable bar.

The blackboard menu above the bar presents a real problem, how to decide from so wide a choice! You could try the nicely presented ploughman's, sandwiches or filled jacket potatoes, or one of the many appetising main meals – the popular steak and ale pie for example. Or you could make an occasion of your visit by eating à la carte in the restaurant. Meals can be ordered any lunchtime or evening (in the bar or the restaurant) with the exception of Sunday evening.

Three real ales are regularly available: Burton's, Benskins and a guest. Drinking hours are normal. Children under 14 can be taken into the restaurant (don't expect bar meal choices or prices there!) or into the garden. Well-behaved dogs can only be taken into the garden.

Telephone: 01707 261384/261267.

How to get there: You will find the Salisbury Crest close to Essendon's parish church, a short distance from the B158. Essendon is signposted where the B1455 leaves the A414 midway between Hertford and Hatfield. Turn right from the B1455 into the B158 after ½ mile.

Parking: At the front of the pub or in the pub's car park nearby. Alternatively along the roadside by the church – except when services are about to be held.

Length of the walk: 4 miles. Map: OS Landranger 166 Luton, Hertford and surrounding area (GR 273088).

From the elevated heights of Essendon the walk dips into lovely valley fields which, for the sake of the wildlife, are normally left uncultivated. It passes the popular Candlestick pub at West End and descends to the river Lea, finally returning to Essendon across fields and along a quiet country lane.

The Walk
On leaving the Salisbury Crest turn left and left again into a footpath behind the pub. This is signposted to Essendon West End and takes you alongside the pub's garden to a gate by the churchyard. Cross the meadow here half-right (210°) to a stile in the far right-hand corner, then go a few steps forward to another stile and into another meadow, ignoring a gate on the left adjacent to the two stiles.

Follow the left-hand edge of the second meadow to a stile; then cross yet another meadow half-right, aiming for a stile behind a fenced pit on the opposite side (190°). After crossing the stile turn right and follow a path straight on downhill. This will take you in and out of a wood to a footbridge at the bottom of the valley. Continue forward and uphill along a field edge to a hedge gap at the top.

Go through the gap and turn left in a tree-shaded bridleway, then right after 25 yards into a path signposted to West End. Soon pass through another gap (or over a stile) and into the light of day. Turn right here and follow two right-hand field edges (as near as the vegetation permits) to the garden of the Candlestick pub, West End.

On leaving the pub's garden, cross to a no through road opposite and go along this for ¼ mile, passing Flint Cottage on the way. When confronted by a 'private' metal gate, turn right into a track just beyond an attractive semi-detached house. Passing a pond on the left at the start, follow the meandering track for ¾ mile until you meet more houses lower down. The track becomes a tarmac road at this point and takes you all the way down to the river Lea, which is hidden by trees near a sharp left turn in the road.

Leave the road here by turning right into a path labelled 'Lea Valley

59

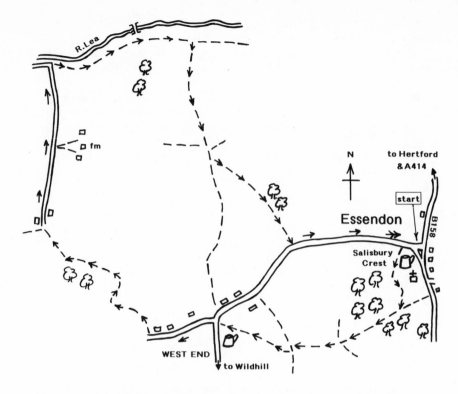

Walk', a 50-mile path along the river Lea from its source at Luton to the river Thames in London. We use ½ mile of this path by following the river alongside its shield of trees.

Soon after passing (not crossing) a wide river bridge, enter a field ahead and follow its right-hand edge, making your exit through a gap at the far end. Do not go forward into the next field, but turn right into a wide track that climbs gently between hedges and trees.

After ⅓ mile you will pass a track which leaves from the right and heads towards farm buildings, and soon after this another which enters fields on the left. Do not go into either of these but continue forward for 25 yards only, while looking for a waymark post in the hedge on the left. Strike across the field half-right (assuming your back is to the hedge), and aim for the distant woodland (130°). This should take you to a waymarked hedge gap 50 yards to the right of the field's far corner.

Continue in the same direction in the next field, cutting off a large field corner and meeting the wood edge by a waymark post. Turn half-right here and follow the wood edge until it terminates; then continue in the same direction across the field (160° and in line with the wood edge) to a stile at the left-hand end of a wide hedge gap. Just to confuse you, there is a footpath signpost at the other end of the gap. No matter: either exit will place you on the Essendon road, and a left turn followed by a hill climb will see you back at the Salisbury Crest.

As you end the day by taking a stroll around the village, notice an inscription on the south-facing wall of the parish church. This commemorates the rebuilding of part of the church after it was bombed by a German Zeppelin airship in 1916. Cottages nearby were also damaged and two villagers lost their lives, a fate shared by the crew of the 'Zeppy' when it was brought down 4 miles away at Cuffley.

⑭ Bayford
The Baker Arms

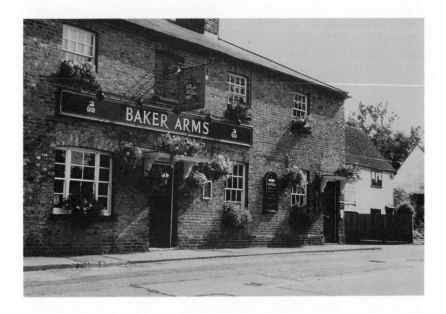

When you come away from the Baker Arms you will realise, as I did, that you have discovered one of the gems of Hertfordshire. And if you enjoy good food (and are happiest when you are not paying the earth) you will want to return again and again. There are three menus: the lunchtime menu, the blackboard menu, and (where you will pay just a little more) the evening menu. All the food on the blackboard menu is home cooked. There are so many items to choose from that you are really spoilt for choice.

Both the young and the old are catered for. Your children may join you inside for a meal and on Monday or Tuesday lunchtime granny and grandpa can feast on a 'Pensioner's Special'. Fido is not forgotten either as he can be taken into the public bar. This is a McMullen's pub, so it follows that McMullen's real ale – Original AK and Country Best Bitter – is on sale, together with their Special Reserve. Drinking hours are normal.

Before moving off to the next pub and the next walk you could spend the night at the Baker Arms, in one of the six quality en suite bedrooms.

Telephone: 01992 511235.

How to get there: If coming from nearby Hertford turn left into Bayford Lane from the B158 about 200 yards beyond the entrance to the University of Hertfordshire Field Station. The pub is 1½ miles along Bayford Lane. Bayford railway station is ⅓ mile from the pub. Turn right as you come out of the station. Trains run from London (Moorgate) hourly, Monday to Friday. On Saturdays and Sundays they run hourly from Kings Cross.

Parking: In the pub's own car park or along the roadside nearby.

Length of the walk: 4½ miles. Map: OS Landranger 166 Luton, Hertford and surrounding area (GR 311084).

A walk containing much that is typical of Hertfordshire: gently undulating countryside with scattered woodland; cultivated fields and meandering brooks; noble houses, humble cottages and beautiful well-kept churches. So much in so few miles!

The Walk
Walking left from the Baker Arms along Ashendene Road you will pass an old cottage dated 1640 opposite one of Hertfordshire's 'Top Ten Ponds for Wildlife'. A quarter-mile further along a pair of semis on the right (Nos 46 and 48) are also dated – 1957. Join a track (signposted as a footpath) just after No 48, and when it runs into a field after 150 yards turn left into the footpath proper. This soon meets a stile and places you along the right-hand edge of a field (210° at first). Stay with the hedge as it turns right and leads you to a stile under trees (300°). From here a woodland path crosses a track (after 50 yards) and describes a mini S-bend and then runs downhill to a footbridge over a brook.

From the footbridge go half-left (250°) and uphill in a field to a stile and metal gate and then in the same direction in the next field to another stile and gate. Bear right to follow a hedge up to yet another stile and gate, in sight of Stratton's Folly. Built in 1789 this tower is said to have functioned as a terrestrial observatory for viewing shipping along the river Thames. If you can believe that, you can believe anything! From here a hedge-lined path takes you to the road by Garden Cottage.

Turn right in the road and left over a stile after a few yards; then along the right-hand edge of two fields in succession to Church Road, Little Berkhamsted. The well cared for church of St Andrew is here, also an attractive terrace of timber-clad cottages. Turn right in the road and left at the war memorial; then right after 75 yards into a bridleway signposted 'Hertford Road 1½' by Lavender Cottage.

A short gravel drive is soon left behind as you go forward through

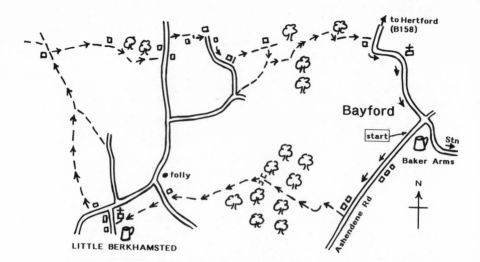

a gate into a field, where a fine view across the Lea valley awaits you. Soon go through another gate to another field and straight on down, with a ditch and the field edge on your left – as well as some magnificent oak trees. At the bottom of the field another path comes in from the right and a signpost directs you over a footbridge (Howe Green) into a narrow bridleway. Since this bridleway is often very muddy, some walkers have resorted to the right-hand field from the outset.

Assuming you are keeping to the bridleway, follow this for ¼ mile until you see barns and a bungalow on the left, then go over a stile on the right a few yards before the bridleway bears left. This will place you in a field with the bungalow and the mud behind you (the same field that 'some walkers' resort to). As you cross the field (80°) you will see Stratton's Folly once again on the hilltop to your right. After walking up and over the field you will find yourself on a grassy track and passing a timber-clad house on your left. Keeping forward in what soon becomes a rough drive you will in due course arrive at a road opposite High Oaks, with a tennis court nearby.

Turn left in the road and soon right into a tarmac drive signposted 'Bayford 1', passing a pumping station at the start. Leave the drive when it runs into a private garden and go forward along a field edge to a stile. Follow a narrow path first right then left and through to another stile after 80 yards. From here a tarmac drive takes you right and becomes a fully fledged lane by Little Stockings.

Just beyond the well-manicured lawns of a large bungalow and where the lane goes off to the right, join the bridleway to Waterhall

64

on the left. This soon curves right and uphill between fields and trees, passes a pond and a tennis court and comes out at a crossing near a collection of one-time farm buildings. Turn right here along a gravel drive and left over a stile (for Bayford) after 100 yards. Keep to the left-hand edge of a field to its bottom left-hand corner (80°) where there is a pedestrian gate and stile. Once through to the adjacent field cut across its corner (30°) for about 50 yards to a stile under trees.

Cross a footbridge under the trees and ignore all paths except the one with a seat and a flight of steps. These steps will take you straight on uphill to a stile and into the open. Keeping close to the trees at the start, cross the field there (70°) straight on and further uphill to its far side, where there is a three-way signpost. Turn right and follow a hedge (140°) to its end; then go through a wide gap to another field and aim for a cottage (Ash Spinney) on the opposite side (90°). Bayford church will be in view slightly right as you proceed.

All being well you will pass along a short path to the left of the cottage. Turn right in the road here and follow it past the church and back to the Baker Arms. If you have time and inclination do call in at the church and see the board giving 'fees to be taken by the minister, clerk and sexton' for services rendered at baptisms, weddings and funerals. You will also see a number of memorials to members of the Baker family, a name which lives on in today's pub. In the churchyard can be found the grave of William Yarrell, a notable 19th century naturalist. This is within a railed enclosure containing other members of the Yarrell family.

15 Wormley West End
The Woodman

To the casual observer the fact that the Woodman is a listed building may seem less significant than its situation on a quiet country road and with a garden enjoying lovely views across trees and fields. This is a comfortable, beautifully maintained pub, matched by the welcoming staff and by the 'fine range of traditionally brewed beers and lagers' and the 'excellent home-cooked food'. In addition to McMullen's Original AK and Country Best Bitter, seasonal and guest beers are usually available. They can be enjoyed at normal pub hours Monday to Friday and Sunday, or all day Saturday (11 am to 11 pm) all year round.

As well as the more usual pub food (ploughman's, burgers, lasagnes and so on) the menu includes some interesting dishes designed to set the gastric juices in motion: gamekeeper pie; leek, potato and mushroom crumble; pork chop in apple and cider sauce. In winter this essentially English menu is reduced slightly to make way for a number of Chinese and oriental dishes.

Children should be happy with the small selection of items that are just for them, but they might insist on finishing off with one of the adult size sweets. If under 14 they can only be taken into the garden.

Dogs are not allowed inside the pub. The menu is unchanged Monday to Saturday lunchtimes and evenings and Sunday lunchtime. Weather permitting a barbecue is set up on Sunday evenings during the summer.
Telephone: 01992 463719.

How to get there: The pub is 2 miles west of Wormley in West End Road. The most straightforward approach is northwards along the A1170 after it leaves the A10 near Cheshunt. From the A1170 at Wormley turn left into Church Lane just beyond the Queen's Head pub; then follow the road signs to Wormley West End (first left then straight on).

Parking: In the pub's car park or along the no through road ¼ mile into the walk. Alternatively park in the East or West Car Parks in Broxbourne Wood, further into the walk (see sketch map).

Length of the walk: 3 ¼ miles. Map: OS Landranger 166 Luton, Hertford and surrounding area (GR 337060).

This walk samples the marvellous expanse of countryside occupied by Broxbourne Woods. As you walk the peaceful bridleways through these woods it is difficult to imagine yourself so close to Hoddesdon and the densely populated area along the Lea valley.

The Walk
Go left along the road from the Woodman, and when this soon turns right keep forward into a no through road. Before ¼ mile is up (and soon after passing cottages on the left) look for a footpath signpost on the right labelled 'White Stubbs Lane ¼'. A kissing-gate here will place you in an uphill path and this in turn into the corner of a field. Follow the field's right-hand edge uphill and go over a stile placed centrally at the far end, where a sign introduces Bencroft Wood. This wood is owned by the County Council and is looked after by the Countryside Management Service. It has been described as part of Britain's finest hornbeam coppice woodland.

Coppicing requires the felling of trees almost to ground level. The subsequent growth of sideshoots provides a harvest of poles traditionally used (in the case of hornbeam) in the manufacture of domestic and agricultural tools.

Go straight on through the area of young coppice to a waymark post on the far side (330°); then turn left into a good gravel path and go along this for 25 yards only. Turn right here under the trees and, passing a pond on the right (a lovely spot), follow the path straight on

67

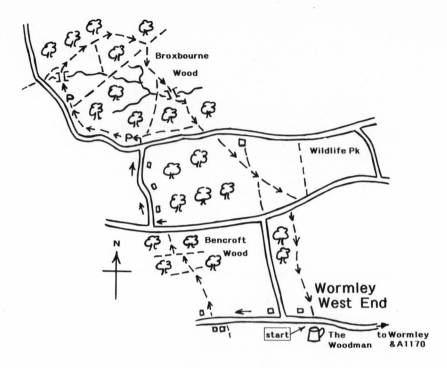

to a road, ignoring all branches as you go.

Turn left in the road and soon right into Pembridge Lane, signposted to Brickendon Green. At a T-junction after ⅓ mile cross to the Broxbourne Wood East Car Park entrance, and by turning left join a bridleway (No 1) that passes behind the car park. With the car park now on your left walk under the trees as far as West Car Park – another lovely spot.

This magnificent wood was purchased by the County Council in 1975 with the help of the Countryside Commission 'in order to maintain its amenity value and to allow public access for peaceful recreation whilst continuing the previous policy of economic forestry' – objectives we should certainly applaud.

Keep straight on from this second car park (do not be tempted into the bridleway leaving from the right) and stay with the path as it curves gradually right to a footbridge. Go right soon after crossing the footbridge (30°), and, ignoring a bridleway leaving from the left at this point, follow the meandering path through the trees. Ignore a 'No Horse Riding' branch on the right as you come out of a shallow dip and soon pass a seat. In due course you will pass another seat before arriving at a meeting of ways.

Cross over the wide bridleway (a straight track extending for two miles through this and other woods) and join another running half-right and downhill (180°) accompanied by a ditch and wire fence on the left.

Now take care! Stay with the track when it turns half-left after 100 yards, but when it soon (50 yards) turns right to go downhill, *keep straight on* through a horse barrier (140°). There is a waymark post here with a white arrow.

The ditch and wire fence continue on your left as you descend to a footbridge. Having crossed the footbridge and turned left immediately, you will be launched into a very meandering path through what you might describe as a jungle (a very nice jungle). You will be guided by white and yellow waymark arrows and assisted underfoot by long stretches of timber planking. You will follow ditches and cross ditches, and eventually emerge at a junction of paths close to a quiet road.

Join the road by going left through a horse barrier; then turn left in the road itself. Walk the road to a stile on the right where the wood gives way to a field. Go into the field and follow its right-hand edge for a few yards to another stile, with the wood on your right.

It is now a matter of walking half-left (assuming your back is to the road) across a succession of five fields, each divided by a stile and some of the stiles daubed with red paint. The actual route is not an exact straight line but zigzags between stiles (varying in direction from 110° to 160°). As you cross the last two fields you may have sight and sound of Paradise Wildlife Park well over to your left, and as you leave the last field from its furthest corner you will arrive at a road.

Turn right in the road and go along this for 60 yards to a path on the left identified by a row of wooden bollards. This is just beyond a field gap and about 100 yards *before* a road junction. Turn left here into a wood, and passing a sign announcing Emanuel Pollards, walk straight on parallel to a field on the left. This will take you to a stile at the far end of the wood. A view across the Lea valley to Epping Forest opens up as you climb the stile into a field and follow the field's right-hand hedge downhill to another stile. Beyond this second stile a narrow path takes you down to West End Lane opposite the Woodman.

Burnham Green
The White Horse

How many visitors to this pub will have come and gone without realising that the horse is headless? It is said that a white horse lost its head hereabouts in a scuffle during the Civil War, and that at night its headless body can be seen galloping down Whitehorse Lane not far from the pub.

There is nothing sombre about the White Horse today. It is a truly attractive pub well-matched by the welcoming staff, the good food and the good drink. The public bar is cosily furnished with traditional settles, while the adjoining restaurant, equally comfortable, leads to the patio and the garden. Children may be taken into the restaurant area, part of which has the attraction of being non-smoking during lunchtime hours.

The reasonably priced lunchtime menu applies every day 12 noon to 2 pm; and you pay the same whether you use the bar or the restaurant. There is a wide choice from simple fare to main meals. If you keep it simple you are more likely to find space for one of the delicious sweets – the sticky toffee pudding, perhaps, or the chocolate, raspberry and hazlenut meringue. The evening menu is distinctly more special (and more pricey), ideal if you have something to celebrate. There are usually about five real ales, with different brews appearing from time to time. Drinking hours are normal. If Fido is with you, I am afraid you will have to leave him outside. Telephone: 0143 879 416.

How to get there: The pub overlooks the green. If you are coming from the A1(M) near Welwyn (not Welwyn Garden City) join the A1000 from junction 6 (Hertford direction) followed by the B1000 Hertford Road (Digswell direction); then turn left into Harmer Green Lane just beyond the magnificent Digswell viaduct. Stay in this road all the way to Burnham Green – even when it changes its name to New Road and back again.

Parking: In front of the pub or alongside the green.

Length of the walk: 4½ miles. Map: OS Landranger 166 Luton, Hertford and surrounding area (GR 262166).

The halfway point of this walk is the delightful river Mimram, and the halfway house Tewin Bury Farm with its restaurant and farm shop. The route follows field and woodland edges but is itself almost entirely out in the open. It enjoys some fine views – at the cost of only two short easy hills.

The Walk
From the White Horse and White Horse Lane go over the road crossing on Burnham Green and into Orchard Road, passing in sight of the Duck, another good hostelry. On the right in Orchard Road you will find the old infant school, now the village hall, and a pair of houses numbered 26 and 28. Go through the gap immediately after the houses and soon cross the short sharp corner of a field (240°). As soon as you enter the next field you should turn left (170°), placing your back to a stile and its complicated waymark post.

Follow the hedge on the left and later, a wood edge on the right. In the far distance Welwyn Garden City comes into view as you descend the hill and go over a stile into the field ahead.

After leaving the wood edge your path keeps straight on, but now across a field (210°) and with a prominent tower block directly ahead. At the next crossing track turn left and soon go uphill through a gap in the trees. In sight over your right shoulder as you ascend the hill is Digswell Viaduct carrying the railway that runs from Kings Cross to the North. It has 40 arches and was built using five million bricks.

The track breaks out into the open and runs down to a crossing (which could be mistaken for a T-junction) where you should continue straight on between the trees. At the next crossing just prior

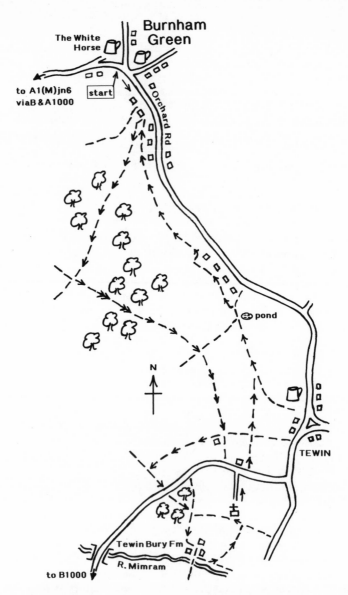

The White Horse

Burnham Green

to A1(M)jn6
viaB&A1000

start

Orchard Rd

N

pond

TEWIN

Tewin Bury Fm

R. Mimram

to B1000

to a cottage turn right so that the cottage and its garden hedge is on your left and a field on your right. From the end of what is a very long hedge keep straight on across the fields (with that distant tower block still directly ahead) to its T-junction with another track. Turn left here and follow a hedge and iron fence to a road. Cross the road to the woodland path opposite and follow this through until you meet a track running along the far side of the wood. Turn right and go downhill in the track and left at the bottom through Tewin Bury Farm, now a hotel, restaurant and farm shop, as well as a farm. Turn right by the farm shop and, passing the old farmhouse, soon arrive at the delightful river Mimram from where the sluices of a former watermill can be seen.

Do not cross the bridge here but turn left and follow a track parallel to the river for 100 yards only. Branch half-left here across the grass, staying in the dip of the hillside and passing about 50 yards left of a small abandoned quarry. Strictly speaking you should follow the dip up as far as a fence and turn left towards St Peter's church and churchyard. Alternatively you could enjoy the freedom to roam that seems to exist here, by taking a more direct route to the church.

Once in the churchyard via its nearest (south-east) corner, you could pass to the east of the church. Here you will find the grave of Lady Anne Grimston who died in 1713 (the units digit on the stone is not clear). She is reported to have said 'If indeed there is life hereafter, trees will render asunder my tomb'. See what you think!

Leave the church along its drive and turn right in the road opposite the imposing Old Rectory, then soon go through a gate signposted 'Upper Green ½' just beyond an attractive timber-framed barn. Cross the field parallel to a fence on the left and aim for a gate at the far end (10°). Having crossed through that gate you could divert to Tewin village if you wish. It has a green, a few nice cottages and two pubs. Simply turn right and soon take one of the two branches into the village.

Back at the stile cross the very large field ahead, maintaining (almost) the same direction as before (360°). This will lead you into a long narrow field and forward again to a lovely tree-lined sunken track (Back Lane) in which you should turn left. You will pass a pond on the right before the track curves right alongside a sports field. When you are halfway round that curve join a narrow path through the trees and scrub on the left and soon turn right at a field edge.

The path follows the backs of well-kept gardens for a while, and after a brief foray to the right crosses open country between fields and with a hedge on the right. It passes a single large oak tree and continues forward, following overhead wires and cutting off a large field corner. After this there are more gardens to accompany you to the road at Burnham Green. Turn left in the road for the White Horse.

17 Stonyhills
The Three Harts

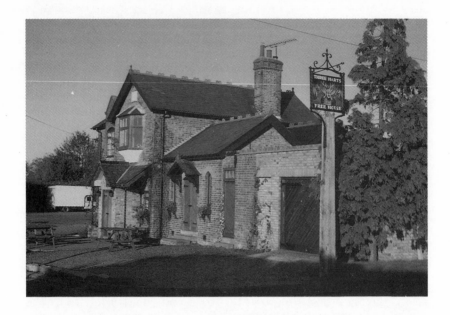

Reserve this walk for a fine, sunny afternoon and return to the Three Harts for an evening meal, then with luck you will enjoy the flaming sunsets for which this pub is renowned. You will certainly also enjoy the food, either from the regular menu or from the specials board. The former includes basket meals, plaice, ham, steak and jacket potatoes; also the traditional ploughman's, salads and sandwiches. Examples from the specials board are lasagne, chicken curry, macaroni cheese and gammon. Except for Sunday evening you can order one of these meals any lunchtime or evening (sunset or no sunset!).

Children can join you inside, also your well-behaved dog. On a warm day you could take them all into the secluded garden at the rear of the pub, and at the same time quench your thirst with Greene King IPA or Abbot Ale, or Ushers Triple Crown. The pub is open for drinking at normal hours only.

Telephone: 01920 463651.

How to get there: Stonyhills, which has just a pub and one or two houses, is signposted from the A119 at Stapleford 2½ miles north of Hertford. Drive through Stapleford and turn left at the first road junction. Alternatively approach from the B158 2 miles north of Hertford along the lane signposted to Chapmore End. After passing the pond at Chapmore End (pond on the right) you should turn left.

Parking: In the pub's car park. Roadside parking is not advised.

Length of the walk: 3½ miles. Map: OS Landranger 166 Luton, Hertford and surrounding area (GR 322169).

A walk that follows more than 1 mile of the lovely river Beane. A marvellous outing for anyone who finds pleasure in trees and shrubs and waterside plants – and who hopes one day to see a kingfisher.

The Walk
From the Three Harts cross the road to a stile and go downhill in a field towards a bend in a narrow lane (270°). On arrival at the lane turn sharp right into a track to Southend Farm Cottage. The 'Private' label should not distract you from the fact that you are on a public right of way.

You may now lay this book to one side while you walk the wide 1 mile track to its meeting with two short (very short) tributaries of the river Beane. Towards the end of this mile you will have passed into the walled estate of Woodhall Park, the house itself having come into view earlier. Although you will need to go through the wooden farm gate on the left just prior to the first bridge (over the first tributary) you may wish to continue in the track a little further for the view, and then come back.

Once through that wooden gate cross the meadow to a kissing-gate (240° and almost doubling back on your previous direction) and continue forward across the grass to the bank of the river Beane. You now have more than a mile of unparalleled delight as you walk alongside this lovely river; but before getting into the swing of it you will need to make your exit from Woodhall Park Estate by climbing over a brick wall. Fortunately a ladder-stile is provided!

The riverside mile is interrupted at the halfway point by the village of Stapleford, where the path runs into a cul-de-sac. Go to the far end of this and turn right at the T-junction, then left along the church drive. Enter the churchyard through a kissing-gate, and, passing to the right of the church, you soon rejoin the riverside path from another gate.

The next ½ mile is marked with numbered posts: stages along a nature trail prepared by the Herts and Middlesex Wildlife Trust. The trail leaflet hints that a kingfisher 'might catch your eye as a spectacular flash of blue'. Such a sighting would make the day complete.

75

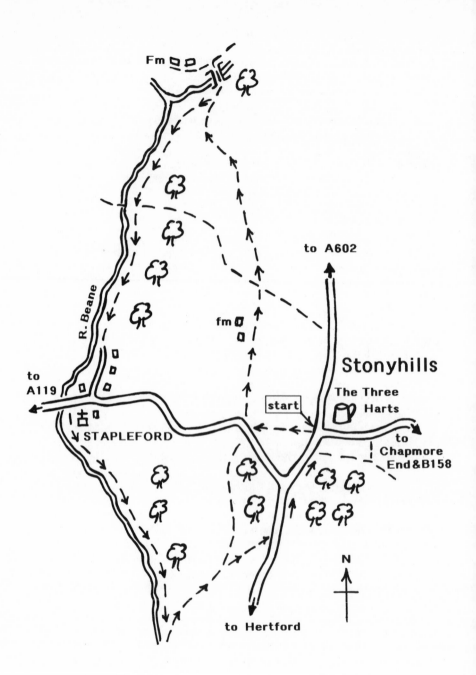

Fm

to A602

R. Beane

fm

Stonyhills

to A119

start

The Three Harts

STAPLEFORD

to Chapmore End & B158

N

to Hertford

The riverside path follows the length of Foxley's Wood before finally emerging into the open, where it turns half-left and runs briefly uphill to meet a tarmac drive. Turn left in the drive – so that the wood is on your left – and stay with it as it leaves the wood edge and runs uphill between fields. When you are midway between one wood and the next (at a left curve in the track and by a 'Strictly Private' notice) leave the drive and cross a field half-right (70°) uphill towards what at first appears to be the right-hand extremity of the second wood.

When you reach the road from the furthest corner of the field go left and follow the road straight on, ignoring a branch on the left to Stapleford and soon arriving back at the Three Harts.

If the day is young, you could drive to nearby Chapmore End. Signposted from Stonyhills, this delighftul hamlet is blessed with a duck pond and a much-liked pub, the Woodman.

Wareside
The Chequers Inn

As the Chequers has recently enjoyed the status of Pub of the Year, bestowed by a local branch of the Campaign for Real Ale, it follows that the choice and quality of the beer from this delightful freehouse is beyond dispute. Equally, there can be no argument about the food or the comfortable old world atmosphere in which it can be enjoyed.

The choice of ales is changed from time to time, and amounts to about six different brews. The wide-ranging regular food menu includes steak, fish, home-made pies, 'Chequers Popular Specials', vegetarian dishes, salads and sandwiches (closed and open). It concludes with a top up of home-made sweets and puddings, cheese-board and liqueur coffees, and just plain coffee and tea. All this every lunchtime and evening, with the exception of Sunday evening. Drinking hours are normal.

Parents with children are asked to eat in the restaurant area, since this is away from the bar. Children cannot be taken into the garden because there isn't one – just a few benches at the front near the road, and not the safest place for youngsters. Dogs may be taken into the bar if well behaved and kept on a lead.

78

You could prepare for another walk by staying overnight at the Chequers, and if your timing is right greet the new day with one of their occasional Scottish breakfasts.
Telephone: 01920 467010.

How to get there: The Chequers is easily found: on the B1004 at Wareside 2 miles east of Ware.

Parking: If the pub's small car park is full, have a word with the landlord of the Chequers, he might be able to arrange access to the adjacent village hall car park. Alternatively park by the triangular green a short distance into the walk.

Length of the walk: 3¾ miles. Map: OS Landranger 166 Luton, Hertford and surrounding area (GR 396156).

If the name 'Wareside' suggests beauty or delight, this walk will not be a disappointment, especially in terms of the valley which Wareside overlooks. This valley is where the meandering river Ash flows, a river that accompanies more than half of the walk.

The Walk
On leaving the Chequers go right along the B1004 and soon right into a lane signposted to Babbs Green. After a few yards you will need to choose either the narrow path immediately to the right of Bourne Cottage or to stay in the lane. The path is for the sure footed and may be overgrown with nettles, but to use it will help to keep it open. If you choose the lane follow it up to a T-junction by Wesley Cottage and turn left. The footpath and the lane join forces near a small triangular green adjacent to a primary school.

From the green go along the lane to the right of the playground, and at the junction ahead (by a pair of half-boarded houses) continue forward in a rough drive. Go left with the drive by another house (and its pond) and forward into a narrow path beyond the next, the third, house. The path runs between hedges and fields and enjoys good views, especially when the leaves have fallen.

In due course the path starts to descend, and is joined by another coming in from the right. It emerges into the open, passes a farm on the left and another on the right, and in the process evolves into a farm track. Ignore a track leaving from the right beyond the second farm and continue forward in the main track all the way to the B1004.

Cross the B1004 to the farm drive opposite and soon turn left along the grass immediately after Waters Place Farmhouse. The grass will soon lead you to a stile and into a field, which you should cross half-

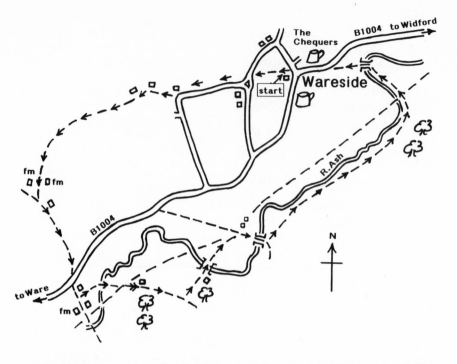

right (80°) towards a footbridge over the river. Having crossed the river continue in the same direction in the next field, aiming at a house on the far slope. Before reaching that house you will cross the trackbed of the former Ware, Hadham and Buntingford Railway, which was closed in 1964 after 101 years of service.

From the trackbed continue in the same direction, passing to the right of the house and to the left of a wood, along a track that progressively steepens. When after 150 yards you reach the near corner of another wood, leave the present track by joining another running downhill on the left (50°). The wood will then be on your right as you descend the hill, and you will pass a cottage when you arrive at the bottom. Stay with the track for a few yards as it curves left beyond the cottage and branch right to a footbridge over the river (your second crossing and two more to go).

Keep straight on from the bridge along a track crossing a field then go right into another track running parallel with the disused railway. When you soon meet yet another track (crossing a railway bridge from the left) go right with it and downhill back to the river. Cross the river and turn left immediately through a gate, then walk the long narrow meadow in sight of a tennis court on the left and guided by two magnificent trees, a horse chestnut and a beech. A stile at the end of the meadow leads into another meadow of similar width, and a gate at the end of this leads into a third, with the river keeping company all the while. Keep to the lowest level of the third meadow (which is overlooked by a wood uphill on the right) and aim for a railway bridge ahead.

After crossing the railway trackbed (immediately to the right of the bridge) and entering the field opposite, walk the river bank as far as a footbridge on the left. Once over the bridge follow the left edge of a field and its accompanying stream (a tributary of the river Ash) back to Wareside and the Chequers.

19 Green Tye
The Prince of Wales

The village of Green Tye need look no further than the Prince of Wales for a pub that complements its community of lovely old houses and cottages. With its colourful summer flowers and attractive garden the pub is a most pleasing sight along the approach road to the village. The licensee goes out of his way to attract walkers. They can be sure of a welcome whether they arrive in ones or twos, or in a party.

The food is good-quality pub fare, nothing exotic but very satisfying and very reasonable priced. Combine this with one of the pub's three real ales (McMullens's Original AK and two guest beers) and it's just the job for a walker's midday lunch. Included in the regular menu is a small selection of main meals, such as shepherd's pie, steak and kidney pie, plaice and scampi. There are also filled jacket potatoes, omelettes, burgers, ploughman's and sandwiches. To round off the meal a choice can be made from hot puddings or ice cream. All this (and a daily specials menu) applies Monday to Saturday lunchtimes and Friday and Saturday evenings.

Normally only cold food is available at Sunday lunchtime. However, hot food can be provided for a walking party by prior arrangement with the licensee. He would also be happy to extend the lunchtime

beyond the usual 2 pm if the party is delayed for any reason. A more extensive range of meals is regularly available on Sunday lunchtimes at the Hoops Inn, Perry Green, 1 mile into the walk. Children are welcome at the Prince of Wales and dogs on leads can be taken inside the pub or in the garden.
Telephone: 01279 842517.

How to get there: Green Tye is best approached from the B1004 3 miles south-west of Bishops Stortford. It is signposted from the B1004 opposite the entrance to Great Hadham Golf Club. The pub is a short distance beyond the green.

Parking: In the pub's car park or alongside the green.

Length of the walk: 5 miles. Map: OS Landranger 167 Chelmsford, Harlow and surrounding area (GR 443184).

This must be one of the most interesting and enjoyable walks in the county. After 1 mile of field edges it enters Perry Green, a village associated with the sculptor Henry Moore. It fords the river Ash (there is a footbridge) and follows part of Much Hadham's fabulous High Street, looping back across delightful river meadows before returning to Green Tye.

The Walk
On leaving the pub turn sharp right immediately into the drive sign-posted (from the roadside opposite) as a public byway. When this runs into a private entrance just beyond thatched Green Tye Cottage, continue forward in a footpath between hedges. At the T-junction ahead turn right and follow a ditch and the right-hand edge of a field, while ignoring a path crossing the field half-left. When confronted by a hedge and another ditch at the far end of the field, turn left and follow the meandering hedge and ditch (on your right), generally heading in the direction of farm buildings.

When close to the farm your path turns right and is joined by another coming in from the left. When it soon goes off to the left (now as a track across the fields) turn right around the second of two ponds and into a field corner (not into the farm drive). Then follow a ditch and hedge on the right all the way along the field (a very long field) to a gap in its far right-hand corner. The gap will place you on Perry Green's green and a left turn in the road (if you so wish) will place you in front of another very nice pub, the Hoops Inn.

From the green cross over to a drive (signposted as a footpath) leading to Danetree House and the grounds of the Henry Moore Foundation. Noting examples of Henry Moore's work on all sides, stay with the drive until it turns left; then go forward across the grass to a stile and into a field. Turn slightly right from the stile (320°) and follow the field edge uphill, passing to the left of a farm and continuing forward across the fields. Do not rush on, but turn right into a path about 50 yards *before* both a stile and the extremity of an infilled gravel working. The path runs between fields divided by a very few trees (10°).

After 120 yards turn left at a path junction (by a tall oak tree) into a wide grassy track leading to a distant wood. On arrival at the wood turn left and follow its edge (wood right, field left) firstly straight on, then round to the right. Leaving the wood behind drop steeply downhill, following overhead wires to a stile at the bottom.

Turn right at a crossing path soon after the stile (i.e. do not go ahead over a footbridge) and follow a path which soon runs just inside the wood (the same wood as previously, but lower down). If you stay on the level and take guidance from the occasional waymark, you will in due course (⅓ mile) arrive at a road. In attempting to avoid mud, some walkers have followed a parallel route deeper in the wood.

Go left in the road, and when it soon turns right keep forward through a metal gate and into a meadow. Maintaining the same direction, cross the meadow to its far right-hand corner (near two 30 mph signs) and go over the stile there. Cross the ford and join a path running uphill opposite. This will eventually place you in Much Hadham's High Street, where you should turn right.

Making your way along the High Street you could hardly fail to notice Forge Cottage (with its museum, Victorian kitchen garden and working blacksmith) and Hopley's Garden and Nursery opposite The Hall. Do have a look at the garden, not only is it very attractive, but entry is free.

When you are almost out of the village take the turning down to St Andrew's church; then tarry in this lovely place. The north side of the churchyard is a good point from which to see the impressive five-gabled palace, for many years the country retreat of the Bishops of London. And inside the church is what must surely be the finest and most varied collection of kneelers anywhere!

Go right with the road by the church and follow it through until it turns right again; then climb a stile in the corner and turn left alongside the garden of Two Bridges. A concrete footbridge will soon place you in a meadow which you should cross more or less straight on (160°). Pass through a kissing-gate in the far left-hand corner and cross a rough drive to the right-hand of two stiles (the one immediately opposite).

The path through the next meadow is fairly obvious and heads in the direction of farm buildings – while the river flows its twisting

84

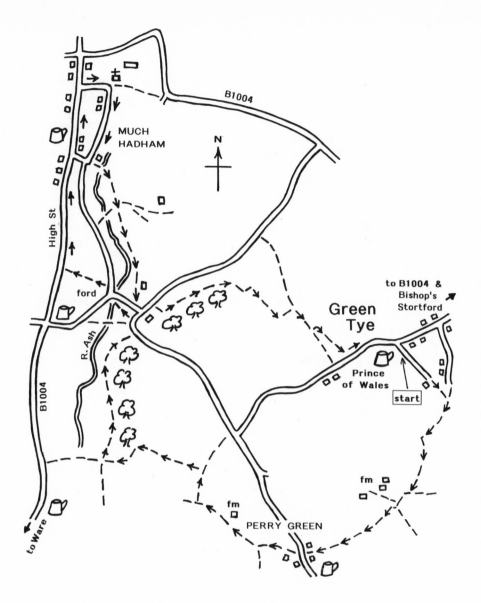

course over to the right. Where the meadow is divided by a stile and fence you should normally go half-right towards the far left-hand corner, where there's a stile and a road (190°); but if you hanker after another look at the ford you could aim for the far right corner of the meadow and join the road there.

From whatever point you join the road turn left in it and left again at a T-junction; then leave the road just beyond a garden and cross a footbridge and stile leading into a field. Go left along the field to a stile at the far end and forward under the trees. The path soon comes out into the open but with the trees still on the right, and it turns right (140°) a few yards before the trees give way to a field. This will soon place you on a field edge higher up, at the mid-point of its shallow dip. Go left here for a few yards to the field corner (by an old oak tree) and then turn right along the grassy boundary between the fields (140°). This all sounds complicated, but in total amounts to no more than an uphill right-hand turn.

When you are confronted by another field higher up (there is no dividing hedge or fence) a few yards before overhead wires, turn left along a grassy path (60°) and, passing under the wires, soon make contact with a track at a T-junction. Turn right in the track and follow this and its accompanying ditch across the fields until you come close to trees on the left.

The remaining stretch of the walk – to the road at Green Tye – runs through those trees parallel to the track and is likely to be muddy and overgrown, and since the entrance to it may not be obvious (just a hole in the trees 15 yards to the left of the track) you could be forgiven for staying in the open as far as the road at Green Tye. Once at the road, turn left and follow this back to the Prince of Wales.

Whitwell
The Eagle and Child

20

The date 1747 inscribed on the outside wall of the Eagle and Child should leave you in no doubt about the age of this freehouse. Inside it is much less apparent just how long the present licensee has held sway here – a quarter century and more. The welcome afforded to customers could hardly have been bettered during all these years, nor the quality of the food. The only problem with the latter is the difficulty in choosing: there are more than 15 hot meals on the menu card and a good variety of cold meals and sandwiches, and all at surprisingly reasonable prices.

Although the menu is on offer only at lunchtimes Monday to Saturday, the licensee is perfectly happy for you to eat your own food (either inside the pub or outside in the garden) when meals are not available, provided you are buying drinks. If however you have arrived completely unprepared at Sunday lunchtime or during an evening you could call instead at the Maiden's Head just along the road, where meals can be obtained at these times.

Real ales are Boddington's, Brakspear's and Flowers IPA, and drinking times are normal. Children are welcome in the End Room if having meals. Dogs may be brought in if kept on a lead. And what may

endear you to this pub more than anything else is that there are no noisy machines.
Telephone: 01438 871280.

How to get there: Whitwell is on the B651 halfway between Hitchin and Harpenden. To connect with the B651 take the B656 from Hitchin or the B652 from Harpenden, via Kimpton.

Parking: In the pub's own car park or along the roadside nearby.

Length of the walk: 4¼ miles. Map: OS Landranger 166 Luton, Hertford and surrounding area (GR 184212).

Not only does this walk start and finish at a most delightful village, but it also traverses some fine Hertfordshire countryside, with good views of the neighbouring hills. It passes through St Paul's Walden where the church has close associations with the Queen Mum. She was baptised here on 23rd September 1900.

The Walk
After turning right out of the Eagle and Child and walking along Whitwell's lovely old High Street, it is interesting to recall a commentary written in 1908 and to know that some things change for the better:

Its situation along the valley of the river is very pretty, but the village itself is unpleasing, being a long row of houses which are for the most part, poor.

From a T-junction by the war memorial keep straight on (for Codicote), and after ¼ mile turn left into a public byway immediately beyond Rose Farm. This track takes you over the river Mimram then slightly left (do not go into the right-hand field here) and uphill. As you tackle the ¼ mile steady climb it would be a serious omission not to glance back at the view of Whitwell and the Mimram valley.

When the track levels out it takes a left-hand turn (not to be confused with a branch leaving ʳfrom the left earlier), and within 100 yards reverts to its previous direction. After a further 50 yards there is an easily missed view (over your left shoulder) of The Bury at the far end of a long avenue of lime trees. The Bury is where Queen Elizabeth the Queen Mother spent part of her childhood and where members of her family (the Bowes Lyons) still live. We will pass close to the house later in the walk.

In less than ½ mile the track joins a lane at a bend. Keep forward here, soon passing East Hall Farm with its pond, ducks and hens. Stay

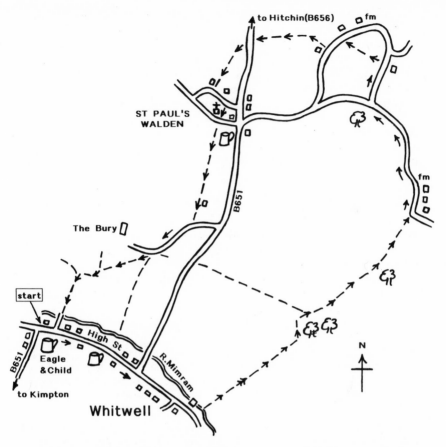

in the lane when it soon curves left (i.e. ignore the farm road going straight on) and continue for ⅓ mile to a road junction where there is another pond. Turn right here (for Shilley Green and Langley) and continue for a further ¼ mile to another junction and yet another pond – the third so far. From this junction go into a track on the left signposted as a footpath. Leave the track almost immediately for a stile and cross a field (300°) to another stile in the field's far left-hand corner to the left of an attractive two-storey cottage.

Turn left in the lane here and go along this for 60 yards to a path on the right. The path passes to the right of a large cottage (almost through its garden, it seems) to a stile. Cross a field to another stile opposite (300° – straight on) and turn slightly left to follow the next field's left-hand edge (270°). When the hedge terminates (by a cattle trough) keep forward across the field (280°) to a stile by the B651.

89

The impressive entrance gates in view half-right as you crossed that field are those of Stagenhoe Park, once the residence of the composer Sir Arthur Sullivan, now a Sue Ryder Home for the physically handicapped.

Cross the B651 (very quiet for a B road) to a path opposite sign-posted 'Whitwell 1¼' and follow this forward (240°) across a field for 40 yards to an electricity pole, then go half-left (200°), aiming for the (largely hidden) church at St Paul's Walden. Three tall trees followed by a hedge accompany the path to a field corner. Keep straight on from this corner alongside a timber fence and in a path that passes a modern house Old Meadow, after which turn left in a lane and right to the church.

Inside the church on the north wall you will find a plaque commemorating the birth 'in this parish' and the baptism 'in this church' of Queen Elizabeth the Queen Mother in 1900. In the tower a 700 year old stained glass window depicts the Virgin and Child, but you will need to peep behind the tower curtain to see the window at its best – against the daylight.

Having passed through the churchyard to the south gate a short diversion may now be made (depending on the state of thirst) to the Strathmore Arms by turning left in the lane.

From the south gate, and with your back to the church, cross the lane to a track opposite (signposted as a footpath) and follow this downhill for ⅓ mile to where it joins a tarmac drive. Just prior to the drive you will have passed Garden House on your left and a lake almost out of sight on the right. Go right and uphill in the drive and cross that magnificent lime avenue – with its view of The Bury – noted earlier in the walk.

Ignore a kissing-gate on the left where the drive starts to curve right (on its way to The Bury) and go through another gate on the left at the completion of the curve, soon after a track comes in from the left, rear.

Now take care! From that second kissing-gate you will need to cross a pasture diagonally corner to corner (240°), aiming for the far end of a line of tall trees, where you may recognise a group of Scots pines. Alternatively aim slightly right of a distant water tower. Turn left into a wide path from that far corner and soon (100 yards) go left and downhill in a sunken track to Whitwell. All being well you should emerge opposite the Eagle and Child.

Nine Wells Watercress Farm at the western end of the village makes an interesting diversion with which to end the day. It has been in the same family for at least 160 years and supplies watercress to Hertfordshire towns and to a London wholesale market – also to passers-by like yourself!

21 Benington
The Bell

Not every Hertfordshire pub can boast such an eminently desirable situation in one of the county's most attractive villages. Well-kept cottages, village pond, church and churchyard face each other across the green, an idyllic scene little disturbed by passing traffic.

The Bell complements and enhances the village with its presence, not least through its welcome and comfort, its good food and its good drink. Whether you prefer simple pub fare or a hot main meal, you can be assured of good quality food in substantial proportions. If you plan to combine your walk around Benington with lunch at the Bell, you could do this any day of the week. You could alternatively walk in the late afternoon and enjoy a meal in the evening, but you must make it Thursday, Friday or Saturday.

Although four real ales are offered (Rayments Special, Greene King IPA, Abbot Ale and XX Dark Mild) this is overshadowed by another much wider choice – 28 malt whiskies.

Children can be taken into the dining-room if having meals, but they would be just as happy in the garden, where they could watch Dad play pétanque. Dogs are allowed inside the pub but not in the garden. Telephone: 01438 869270.

91

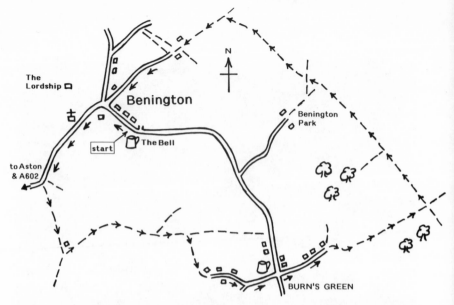

How to get there: If coming from the A1(M) near Stevenage, join the A602 from junction 7 (Stevenage direction, then Hertford direction from the first roundabout) and turn left after 2 miles into Aston Lane at Bragbury End opposite the Roger Harvey Garden World. Follow the road signs to Aston and turn sharp right out of Aston for Benington.

Parking: In the pub's car park or along the roadside if the car park is full.

Length of the walk: 4½ miles. Map: OS Landranger 166 Luton, Hertford and surrounding area (GR 301235).

A walk with two long uninterrupted valley paths, level but enjoying magnificent views – ideal if you are of a mind to step it out and cannot wait to get back to this lovely village! Or it could be that you hope to visit the Benington Lordship Gardens before returning home. They are open in February for the snowdrops and from spring until autumn, Wednesday and Sunday afternoons; also bank holiday afternoons.

The Walk
From the road junction on the green (adjacent to the village pond) go downhill in the Aston direction, passing the parish church on your right. This little-used road can be an open invitation to the occasional reckless motorist, so do please be watchful.

Ignore the first track on the left (the one going forward and uphill near a Benington road sign) and continue to the second. This is 50 yards beyond a stile and gate on the left. Follow this track (a bridleway) between hedges and under electricity wires all the way to a fenced pumping station. At a T-junction in the track here turn left and follow another set of wires along the dip of the fields, with a ditch on the left.

After ⅓ mile the track turns left and runs uphill. Keep straight on here, along a footpath and still following the ditch and the wires. When you arrive at a hedge corner after 200 yards (adjacent to an electricity pole), turn right and go uphill along the field edge (180°) to a stile at the far end of the hedge. Cross the stile into the sharp end of a field and go up towards a cottage, where a metal gate will lead you into a lane. Follow this lane to the road at Burn's Green by the Lordship Arms.

Cross to Hebing End opposite (a no through road) and go with it to its end. You cannot go wrong: there is a pond at the beginning of the road and a pond at the end. When the tarmac terminates just beyond the second pond, turn right into a bridleway running between a field left and a garden right. After 60 yards the track turns left and takes a level route along a left-hand field edge (about 60°). It drops downhill along the next field edge (there is woodland in view beyond the right-hand field edge) to a gap near the bottom of the valley.

Go through the gap to another field and forward to a footbridge *but not over it*. Turn left here so that a ditch is on your right and enjoy this marvellous 1 mile valley walk. It is interrupted twice only: by a private track leaving from the left after ⅓ mile and by an oblique crossing track after a further ⅓ mile. The latter is just beyond a tree-planted triangle and comes down from Benington Park. Continue forward from the oblique crossing and complete the final ⅓ mile along the valley, with the ditch remaining on your right.

Go through a hedge gap at the far end into another field and turn left immediately, then follow the left-hand hedge for 75 yards (230°) and join a track going uphill under trees. Now comes the sting in the tail of this good walk – mud. (The reputation that this track has acquired has led some walkers to take avoiding action by walking along the edge of the right-hand field.) All is forgiven when the track evolves into tarmacked Duck Lane, a name which becomes meaningful when you arrive at the pond in Benington.

㉒ Great Offley
The Green Man

The Green Man's slogan 'open 8 days a week' is not very far from the truth. If you arrive here any time between 11 am and 11 pm Monday to Saturday you can have a bar meal. On Sunday the times are 12 noon to 3 pm and 7.30 pm to 10.30 pm. The licensee is proud of his 'good value food', much of which is prepared on the premises. 'You will not find plastic food here!' he says. The wide range of bar meals – at prices to suit most pockets – can be enjoyed in the bar area or in the light and airy conservatory. You could alternatively eat in the garden, where there is a marvellous view across country. If you wish to make your visit more of an occasion in itself you could dine in the restaurant any day from 12 noon to 3 pm or 7 pm to 11 pm.

The pub is open for drinking virtually all day Monday to Saturday (11 am to 11 pm). On Sunday the usual restrictions apply. Real ales number at least six, with different brews being offered from time to time.

Children are made very welcome, the conservatory or the garden being ideal for them. There is an attractive and safe play area at the

front of the pub. Dogs are also welcome, assuming they are on their best behaviour.
Telephone: 01462 768256.

How to get there: Great Offley is well signposted from the A505 halfway between Luton and Hitchin. Bus 92 to 99 from Hitchin Station runs half-hourly Monday to Saturday, hourly Sunday pm. There is a good rail service daily from London (Kings Cross) to Hitchin. You will find the pub close to the main village crossing.

Parking: In the pub's car park or along the roadside, especially near the church in High Street.

Length of the walk: 4½ miles. Map: OS Landranger 166 Luton, Hertford and surrounding area (GR 142271).

If you have any reservations about the beauty and variety of Hertfordshire's countryside this walk should put them to rest. It commences with a lovely 1¼ mile of quiet lane (a no through road) with some of the county's finest views. After passing Little Offley (a Tudor manor house) it returns to Great Offley through woods and across fields that seem to be on top of the world.

The Walk
From the Green Man go over the crossing into School Lane, not failing to notice the timber-framed dovecote along the farm drive on the left, or the farmhouse. Follow the lane over the bypass and stay with it for ½ mile until it branches two ways – where there are signs in abundance. Take the half-right option, for Wellbury House and Pirton (Little Offley is in sight, along the other branch) and follow this narrow meandering lane for ¾ mile, firstly in the open, then under trees, then downhill and in the open again, almost to Wellbury House.

When you are at the bottom of the hill (shortly before the lane turns right), look for a three-way waymark post beside a brick wall. Turn left here into a level path in the dip of the field and aim for the right-hand extremity of a wood (250°). After you pass the wood edge you should climb the next field straight on in its very steep dip (210°) – not turning left around the wood edge and not forgetting to look back at the view. With the barns of Little Offley in sight ahead, keep forward from the top of the hill along a track on level ground, then skew slightly right and pass between a stable block and a barn.

Continuing in your previous direction, but now along a field edge, you will soon pass the Tudor manor house. Follow the field edge as it curves right, and when it comes out of the curve resume your previous direction by joining a track on the left along a left-hand field

95

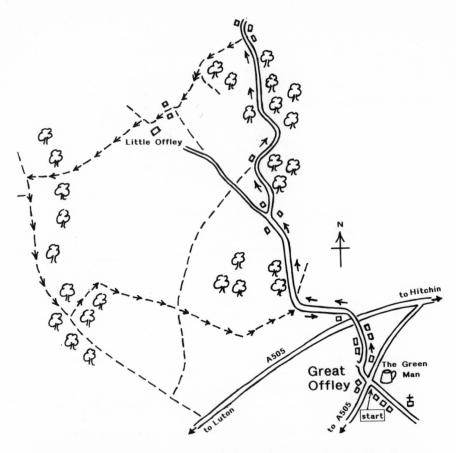

edge (240°). If there is a tall pylon emerging from the trees directly
ahead (distantly), then chances are you are on the right course.

Follow the hedge all the way to the field's far left-hand corner. Once
there enter a wood and trace the meandering path through the
hawthorns to the far side. If there are no waymarks visible follow the
hoofmarks instead (approx 290°)! When you emerge from the trees
turn left and soon cross a field (250°) to a waymark post on the far
side – and feel yourself on top of the world.

Turn left here (south) and follow the right-hand field edge, soon
under electricity wires and straight on. The wood through which you
have just walked will be well over to your left and a panoramic view
(weather permitting) to your right. The space between you and the
trees gradually diminishes as the path progresses, and you will find
yourself beside a short gap between one woodland and the next.

96

Continue forward 30 yards from the gap to a path on the left running into what is a spur of this second woodland; and then start counting! After 250 man-sized paces (200 yards) along this clear path through the wood another path leaves from the left (50°). This path may not be waymarked, but you can identify it by its shortness (100 yards) and the fact that you can see the light of day at its far end.

Having gone along that path you will emerge into a field corner. Continue forward along the field edge, with trees on your immediate right, and then turn right at the wood corner and follow the trees along for 35 yards only. From this point launch slightly left across a field along its dip (110°) to a waymark post at a hedge corner. Keep forward, with the hedge left and fields left and right; then over a crossing by a three-way electricity pylon.

As you follow the overhead wires straight on uphill along the next field edge, the sight and sound of the A505 will become apparent. Soon after this, and on level ground, the field edge curves left and the path (now a track) goes with it, passing between hedges (60°) and eventually meeting a road. If the track at one point is more suitable for ducks than walkers, you could take avoiding action by advancing through the trees on the left. On arrival at the road turn right and make your way back to the Green Man.

23 Pirton
The Fox

The Fox is an exceptional pub in a number of ways: it warmly welcomes walkers and cyclists; it is open for drinking all day (11 am to 11 pm) Monday to Saturday; bar lunches are served every day (including Sunday); and if you happen to arrive in, say, the middle of the afternoon tired and hungry, the cook (the licensee's wife) may well take pity on you.

The menu card includes sandwiches, ploughman's, soup, hamburgers and 'Foxy Yorkies' – Yorkshire pudding with sausages and gravy. The specials board offers a few items for those who prefer something more in the way of a main meal. Do the walk on a Thursday, Friday or Saturday and return here for a meal in the evening, with the option of take-away fish and chips on Friday. Your children may join you (at one of the tables in the games room), and your well-behaved dog need not be left in the car.

Real ales are Boddingtons (Bitter or Mild) and up to three other brews which are changed regularly.

Telephone: 01462 711101.

How to get there: The pub is located in the High Street near Pirton's parish church. If approaching from Hitchin, which is 2½ miles south-east of Pirton, join the B655 (from the A505) and branch right into an unclassified road after 1 mile.

Parking: In the pub's large car park or along the roadside nearby. You could alternatively park at Great Green. This is near Pirton's other two pubs and a short distance along the walk.

Length of the walk: 4¼ miles. Map: OS Landranger 166 Luton, Hertford and surrounding area (GR 147318).

The four superlatives that passed through my mind when I first walked this route were: 'great fields, great woods, great views, great walk.' Choose a fine day and you could well experience the same emotions – assuming that you are happy with the long steady ascent that marks the first half of the walk.

The Walk

From the Fox cross the High Street to Crab Tree Lane opposite and soon go right with this (so that the church is on your left), following the road through to Great Green. Here you will find Pirton's other two pubs. With the Green (the grassy part) on your right stay in the road to its junction with Hitchin Road/Priors Hill. When you cross this to the track opposite (beside a transformer and signposted 'Pegsdon 1') you are at the start of a marvellous uninterrupted ascent taking you to a height of 400 feet in 1 mile. Included in the view as you climb is the church at Shillington prominently sited on a mound and the space-age radio listening station at Chicksands, Bedfordshire; also a prehistoric burial mound in sight after you pass a wood on the right.

The termination of that 1 mile climb coincides with the far end of a stretch of woodland on the left. Here a waymark post marks the division of the route into two, and if you continue forward a few more yards you have the prospect of a very fine view westward across Hexton and the Burton Hills in Bedfordshire. Back at the waymark post you should take the left-hand branch in the track and follow a hedge and overhead wires to the B655 road.

Cross the road to a wide track signposted to Great Offley and New Wellbury Farm. Deacon Hill makes its appearance ½ mile westward as you ascend the gently sloping track and approach Woodland Cottage. Beyond the cottage a stretch of woodland hides farm buildings and leads you forward towards a T-junction. Just before the junction a waymark arrow on the left directs you through the trees and alongside an iron fence to a stile. Go forward between farm buildings (New Wellbury Farm), then between fields and uphill in

99

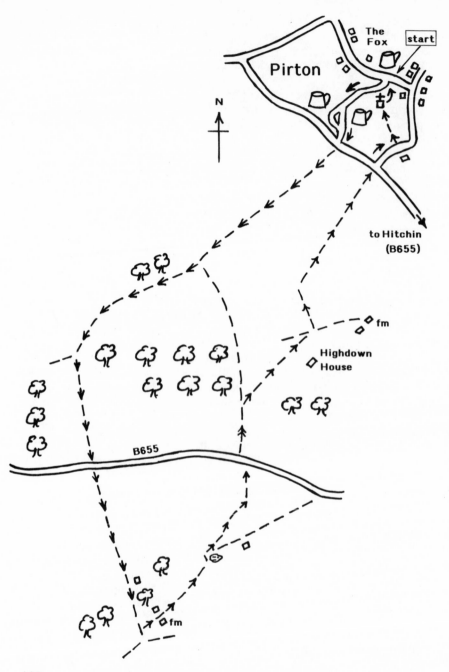

The Fox

start

Pirton

N

to Hitchin
(B655)

fm

Highdown
House

B655

fm

a wide grassy track (40°), passing a water-filled pit on the right at the top.

The track soon turns left then right, skirting a pond on the right and meeting a stile adjacent to an electricity pole. A little concentration is now required. Do not be tempted into the track running forward from the stile along the right-hand field edge, but cross the field itself about quarter-left with respect to the track (40°). You will pass about 25 yards left of a double pole electricity pylon, with a farmhouse downhill beyond that.

When you arrive at a field corner (Hitchin is distantly in view half-right), bear left and, *without leaving the field*, follow the right-hand hedge (0°). You will pass some yards right of an overgrown pit before being led downhill to a road. Turn left in the road and right after 40 yards into a field. Descend the dip of the field and climb the steep slope opposite, following the left-hand hedge to a stile at the top and into another field.

Your utmost concentration is required yet again! Cross the field roughly halfway between the left-hand wood and the right-hand house (40°). This direction is a little right of Pirton church, now coming into view ahead, and will take you within 150 yards of the house. Much of this lovely stone-built house (High Down) dates back to the late 1500s or thereabouts. Notice the ornate weather vane, it may help you in getting the correct bearing across this field.

As you pass the house go downhill to a stile where four fields join (not the 'private' stile), then cross a farm track to the left-hand edge of a field, with a hedge left (340°). The rest is easy. Follow the hedge (the church is half-right now) to its far corner by an electricity pole which has wires branching three ways. Turn right here and follow the wires and the left-hand hedge down to Hitchin Road.

Join Walnut Tree Road opposite and stay with this as far as a gate on the left opposite Walnut Tree Farm. Cross the undulating ground from the gate and make your way towards the church and its south gate. The fact that the church was built on the site of a Norman castle explains the profile of the ground here. The castle keep stood on Toot Hill, the mound near the churchyard's south-west corner. Once in the churchyard turn right and soon find yourself in Crab Tree Lane opposite the Fox.

㉔ Weston
The Thatched House

If you are looking for a friendly village pub, where the food is very nicely cooked and where it does not cost the earth, you could hardly do better than the Thatched House, Weston. The choice of food is more than adequate for a walker's lunchtime needs, with a selection of hot items including home-made steak and kidney pie, mixed grill, fish and chicken – and the best chips you will find anywhere. There are also filled jacket potatoes, burgers, ploughman's, sandwiches and soup. On Sundays you also have the option of a traditional roast lunch. Drinking hours are normal except on Saturdays, when the pub is open all day (11 am to 11 pm). Real ales are McMullen's Country and AK and two guest beers.

Children under 14 can only be taken into the garden. The same restriction applies to dogs, perhaps because the pub is already occupied by an Alsatian, who gives a harmless barking welcome to the first customer following opening time.

Telephone: 01462 790273.

How to get there: If you are coming via the A1(M) join the A6141 near Letchworth (in the Baldock direction) and soon turn right into the B197, then first left for Weston. Once at Weston (by the Red Lion) turn right into Damask Green Road, but do not look for a thatched pub – it isn't!

Parking: In the pub's car park or along the roadside.

Length of the walk: 3¾ miles. Map: OS Landranger 166 Luton, Hertford and surrounding area (GR 258298).

This walk starts with a mini tour of the best of this delightful village – its tiny green and pond, its thatched houses and its well-kept cottage terraces. It passes through the idyllic precincts of the parish church before crossing fields to Hall's Green, and returns to Weston across a series of lush green meadows.

The Walk
From the Thatched House go left along Damask Green Road to the Red Lion, then straight on along Fore Street, with the green and its pond on your right. About 100 yards before the White Horse Pub (which is at a road junction) join a rough drive on the right signposted to Maiden Street. This drive soon runs into a footpath which passes between lovely cottage gardens to a road.

Turn left in the road and follow this downhill to where it narrows; then turn right into a drive just beyond a school. When the drive soon terminates continue forward, but now along a footpath between hedges. This passes a pair of almshouses and runs between fields to the churchyard gate. You may find the church more interesting inside than out, the most striking feature being the group of four Norman arches over the choir stalls.

As you leave the churchyard's east gate turn right in the church drive and very soon left into a footpath signposted 'Halls Green 1' immediately beyond Glebe Cottage. Follow the cottage hedge for just a few yards before crossing a field half-right (140°) aiming at the right-hand end of a wood ¼ mile ahead. This path will take you into a dip and across a ditch, then slightly right and uphill towards an electricity pole at the top. Looking back see what a fine picture the church and cottages make.

Go through a hedge gap by that pole and continue forward, now following overhead wires and about 75 yards to the right of the aforementioned wood. Stay with the wires in and out of another dip and over a drive, then across a field followed by a small pasture. Cross the next field (the last, for the time being) straight on to its corner (without the wires), aiming for the Rising Sun pub sign by the road at

103

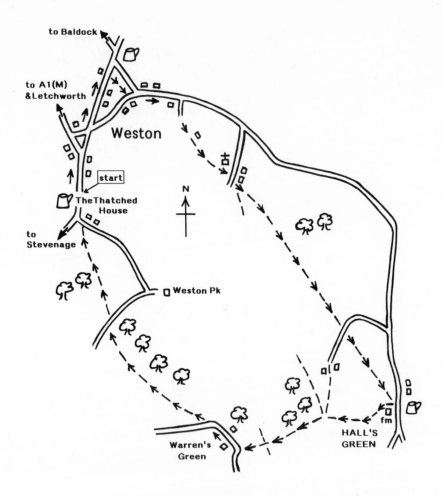

Hall's Green. Do not join the road (unless attracted by the Rising Sun) but turn right from the field corner along a wide farm drive, passing to the right of farm buildings. Soon go half-left (diagonally) across the yard to a track leaving from its corner and follow this across fields and alongside trees. Go left with the track from a junction of ways and, with a wood on your immediate right, stay the course for ⅓ mile until you meet the road at Warren's Green.

Turn right in the road and go along this to where it turns left. Leave the road here by going forward through a kissing-gate and along the short left edge of a small meadow. When a stile soon places you in a larger meadow you should go slightly left (290°) to pass 20 yards left of an ancient oak tree; then more or less straight on across what turns out to be a series of stiles and meadows, eventually (⅓ mile) walking alongside the wood on the right.

Cross a tarmac drive to a kissing-gate and walk the edge of the right-hand field straight on to a stile in the far left-hand corner, passing close to a wood edge as you go. If the stile invites you into a bed of nettles it would be sensible to climb the gate a little to the right of this. Both exits lead on to a tarmac drive where you should turn left. A few yards along the drive and you are back in Damask Green Road, where a right turn will take you back to the Thatched House.

㉕ Buntingford
The Fox and Duck

Situated in what must be Buntingford's most attractive street, close to the river Rib and amongst lovely houses and terraced cottages, the Fox and Duck has a very welcoming appearance from the outside. Inside, that welcome is confirmed, and along with the comfort of the bars, makes this a very nice pub in which to round off the day.

Although the licensee speaks of the Fox and Duck as a drinker's pub, eaters would certainly find it much to their liking. The regular menu lists sandwiches, filled jacket potatoes, toasties, ploughman's, hot snacks and hot food (fish, chicken, ham, sausages and the like). This is expanded by a number of dishes on the changing blackboard menu. You can eat in the public bar or in the relatively quiet and more relaxing lounge bar; but for this you must come here Monday to Saturday lunchtime only, because no food is served on Sundays or in the evenings. You could bring your own food at Sunday lunchtime and eat this in the garden (the licensee is agreeable) or have a Sunday roast (only) at the Bull in High Street.

Drinking hours are 11 am to 11 pm on Monday, Friday and Saturday, and normal on other days; so there is plenty of opportunity to imbibe the Greene King ales – IPA, Abbot Ale and XX Dark Mild

– or the draught Red Rock cider.
Children under 14 can only be accommodated in the garden (a patio at the back of the pub). Well-behaved dogs may be brought inside – but only one at a time, please!
Telephone: 01763 271308.

How to get there: The pub is in Church Street and is not easy to find if coming by car. The best advice is to leave your car in the High Street free car park. This can be reached from two points on the A10(T); the shortest is from the junction of the A10(T) with the A507. Take the Buntingford branch here and turn left after ⅓ mile into Bowling Green Lane. From the car park walk under the town clock and over High Street into Church Street.

Parking: In the pub's small car park (space for eight cars only) or in the High Street car park; see above.

Length of the walk: 4¼ miles. Map: OS Landranger 166 Luton, Hertford and surrounding area (GR 362296).

This walk samples a little of Hertfordshire's wide open spaces. Apart from stopping to see the roofless church at Layston and the manor house, church and farm at Wyddial, there is little to slow the pace, leaving time for a leisurely amble around the pleasant town of Buntingford.

The Walk
From the Fox and Duck cross the river bridge and walk through the huddle of cottages to The Causeway, a no through road. Turn right in this (there is a school sign here) and go uphill in what soon becomes a lovely quiet lane. After ¼ mile the lane twists and turns and meets a large white house on the right. You may have already glimpsed the roofless church behind the trees ahead. We will be passing the church towards the end of the walk and can postpone our visit until then.
Turn right into the grassy track between the house and a grey corrugated barn and follow the track across fields (70°). There may not be a waymark or signpost to guide you; all you have is my word! The track soon curves left, then right to resume its original direction. It passes through a hedge gap (over a ditch), and across more fields to a T-junction. Turn left here into another good grassy track along a shallow dip in the fields (50°), following a deep ditch on your right. After going left with the track you should ignore a branch leaving from the right, then continue forward, soon walking alongside a wood and guided by low voltage electricity wires.
After passing under a line of high voltage wires go left with the track

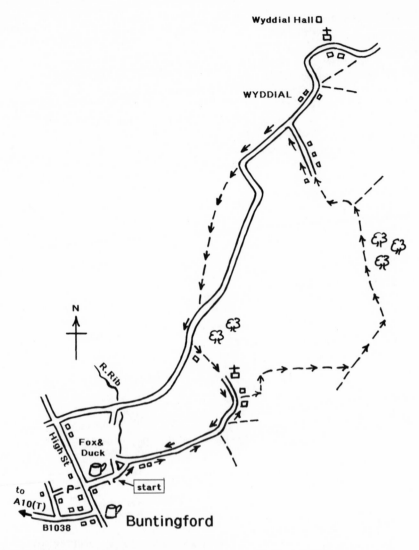

Wyddial Hall

WYDDIAL

N

R.Rib

Fox&
Duck

to
A10(T)

B1038

start

Buntingford

(there may be a bridleway signpost at the bend, pointing back to Buntingford) then soon right, resuming your previous direction. The track becomes a tarmac drive by Moles Farmhouse and takes you to the road at Wyddial. Now is your moment of decision: you could turn right in the road, and walk ⅓ mile to Wyddial church and back. In addition to the church you would also see 18th century Wyddial Hall and the magnificent timber-framed Wyddial Bury Farmhouse. If that does not appeal turn left in the road and skip the next paragraph.

Wyddial Hall can be seen from the north side of the churchyard. Looking back from this point you will notice that the north aisle of the church is entirely (and unusually) in brick. This is Tudor brick, dated 1532. You will almost certainly find the church locked, and so your chances of appreciating to the full its eight panels of 16th century Flemish glass is somewhat remote! You can however appreciate the lattice-paned windows of the terrace of Victorian cottages as you retrace your steps through the hamlet.

When the road turns left after ¼ mile look for the second of two footpath signposts. Labelled 'Buntingford 1½' this sign is just around the bend and directs you forward (in the same direction as previously) along the left side of a ditch (210°). Do not be tempted to walk along the other side, unless you have very long legs and can jump the ditch when it proves necessary!

Stay with the ditch for very nearly ½ mile, until you are back on the road; then go forward in the road for about 150 yards to an S bend. When you are halfway into the S go uphill in a track on the left. This takes you up to the roofless church of St Bartholomew.

The church may have served a medieval village called Ichetone, which was probably deserted in favour of the more prosperous Buntingford. Services are still held here, but only occasionally: a Christmas carol service is one example. The churchyard is delightfully wild and can be entered through a hedge gap where the track changes to a tarmac lane. It is possible to leave the churchyard along a short path that runs parallel to the lane, rejoining the lane further along. All that now remains is an easy amble along the lane back to Buntingford.

As you re-enter Buntingford notice that the restored Lock Up (between the river and the Fox and Duck) stands in readiness, complete with bed, candle, plate and tankard.

Furneux Pelham
The Star

If you are not the sort to be governed by the clock (especially on your day off) and are likely to need a meal well outside the conventional hours, this lovely old pub should suit you very well. Its kitchen is primed for action at exactly the same times as the bar: 11 am to 3 pm and 6 pm to 11 pm Monday to Friday, 11 am to 11 pm Saturday, 12 noon to 3 pm and 7 pm to 10.30 pm Sunday.

The hot meals are very substantial affairs and come under four different headings – potted meals, basket meals, vegetarian meals and main meals – together presenting a wide range of choices. On a warm sunny day one of the salads or ploughman's would make a refreshing start to the walk, especially if eaten in the garden along with a glass of the Greene King real ale.

Judging by the huge pile of logs stacked in readiness at the end of the building (in view from the toilet window) this is a good pub in which to spend an hour or two when the weather is not so warm and sunny. That might also be a good time to order one of the all day breakfasts – a real bargain.

Since children can only be taken into the garden, families will need to come here on a warm day. Well-behaved dogs are catered for with a welcoming bowl of water.

Telephone: 01279 777712.

How to get there: The Star is close to St Mary's church at the western end of the village. A straightforward approach is from the A120 at Little Hadham three miles west of Bishops Stortford. Take the road signposted to 'Albury and the Pelhams' and carefully follow road signs to Furneux Pelham (4 miles). At the second turning take the 'Ferneux Pelham & Braughing' option. The pub can also be approached from the A10 via Buntingford.

Parking: In the pub's car park or by St Mary's church.

Length of the walk: 5 miles. Map: OS Landranger 167 Chelmsford, Harlow and surrounding area (GR 431279).

In addition to visiting the delightful Patmore Heath nature reserve at Gravesend, this walk enjoys some excellent views across the Hertfordshire countryside. The surface along some of the paths is uneven, and their covering of grass may well be wet, so you will need to be sure footed and well clad at the very least.

The Walk
The walk starts from a footbridge at the rear end of the pub's car park. Once over this cross the grass to a stile leading into a field; then turn left immediately and follow the field edge into the corner. Ignore a stile on the left of the corner and go over another directly ahead. You now have a succession of three field edges to accompany you all the way to a road (180° straight on).

Turn left in the road and follow it uphill to a footpath on the right. This is signposted 'Gravesend ½' (a short measure, to be sure!) and leaves the road 40 yards before a junction, where stands a very fine thatched cottage. This footpath (a grassy track at the start) crosses the fields (150°) and presents an impressive all-round view of Hertfordshire, marred only by the power distribution centre 2 miles away near Stocking Pelham.

A footbridge at the far end of this very long field will take you over a ditch (the river Ash, in fact) and into another field. You should cross this second field in exactly the same direction as previously, climbing the hill and meeting a road at the top. Turn right in the road and walk into Gravesend as far as the Catherine Wheel pub. Turn left into the narrow lane here and go uphill to the Patmore Heath Nature Reserve.

Leased to the Herts and Middlesex Wildlife Trust, the reserve is one of the finest pieces of heathland left in Hertfordshire. Although our walk takes us into the first turning on the right by the near corner of the reserve, in order to see this at its best it is necessary to stay in the lane a little longer, and then come back.

Back at the corner of the reserve and going along the road between

111

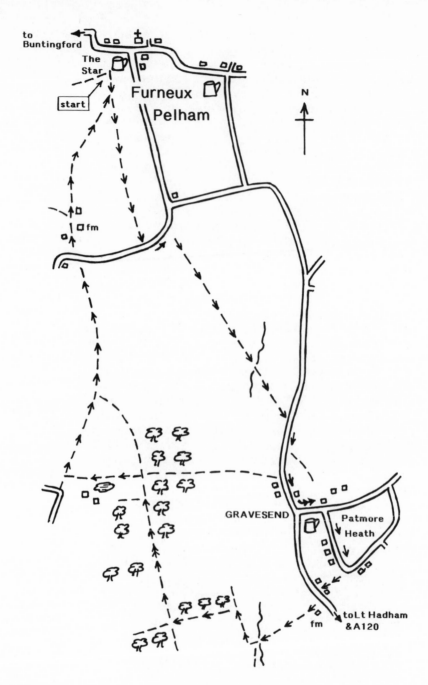

to
Buntingford

The
Star

start

Furneux
Pelham

N

fm

GRAVESEND

Patmore
Heath

to Lt Hadham
& A120

fm

the reserve (left) and the houses (right), stay with the road until it turns left around a pond. Cross the grass here in front of timber-clad Hitch Lane Cottage and join a path on the right between hedges. When this soon divides take the right-hand branch and follow this good path downhill and back to the main road.

Turn left in the road and very soon right into a farm track (a bridleway) by High Hall Farmhouse. Keep straight on and downhill to a ditch at the bottom, following overhead power lines all the way. Cross the ditch and stay in the track for a further 75 yards, turning right with it once you have crossed another, lesser, ditch. With this ditch now on your right, you will be heading for the lower end of a line of trees and bushes (350°). Turn left when you get there (150 yards) and follow the trees uphill (trees on your right) to a waymark post at a crossing in the top right-hand field corner.

Turn right at the crossing and, with a young plantation on your left initially, follow this good track soon downhill then steeply up towards the left-hand border of a wood. Now take care: ignore a branch on the left before you reach the far end of the wood, then keep straight on (along what is now a less than even surface) for about 50 yards to a crossing where the wood *does* end.

After turning left here (280°) and crossing a field, you will pass to the right of a large well-stocked pond, followed by a house. Turn right at a T-junction when you arrive at a second (smaller) pond, and soon find yourself walking parallel to a hedge on the left. Furneux Pelham's church will be in view as you descend a dip in the fields (360°) to a footbridge at the bottom. If in doubt aim in the direction of the left-hand of two distant white cottages.

By climbing the opposite slope straight on between fields you will, after ¼ mile, arrive at a road. Turn left in the road and right after only 30 yards into the rough drive (a bridleway) to Patient End Farm. You will pass the lofty red brick farmhouse and a low (equally red) farm building with a pantiled roof, before crossing a stile and entering a field ahead. Keep straight on along the left-hand edge of the field to a metal gate in the corner, then make your way to a stile 30 yards to the right of the next field's far left-hand corner, beyond the right-hand extremity of a knot of trees. Go half-right downhill (40°) in the next field to a stile in its furthest corner. Now go forward along the edge of the final field to a stile on the right, and there is your pub.

Before returning home note the time on the church clock – but do not ask why – and do take one last look at this delightful corner of Furneux Pelham.

27 Ashwell
The Rose and Crown

The Rose and Crown takes full advantage of its prime position in one of Hertfordshire's most attractive villages by the welcome afforded to its customers and by the quality and variety of its food and drink. So long as you do not arrive on a Monday (the cook's day off) you have an excellent range of meals to choose from. There is the regular hardcopy menu of meals and snacks in addition to dishes of the day on the blackboard, which might include the intriguing Butler's Pie and Harvester's Pie.

The weight-conscious can choose from at least five salads, while those less concerned with their figures can tuck into something like a steak and kidney pie and follow this with one of seven puddings or eight varieties of ice-cream. Or they could come here on Fish and Chip Day (Tuesday) or Sausage and Mash Day (Thursday), with sausages from the nearby village of Hinxworth. Food is available Tuesday to Sunday lunchtimes and evenings, except Sunday evenings, but with a slightly reduced choice on Sunday lunchtime.

Real ales are Greene King IPA, Rayments Special Bitter and Abbot Ale, drinking times being normal. The dining-room is ideal for children and non-smokers. Organised walking parties are very

welcome, but prior warning of an invasion would be appreciated! Dogs may only be taken into the garden.
Telephone: 01462 742420.

How to get there: Ashwell is signposted from the A505 3 miles north-east of Baldock. Turn left when you reach Ashwell's High Street; the pub will then be on your left. Ashwell and Morden Station is near the A505, 2 miles by road from the village. Trains from London (Kings Cross) run twice hourly Monday to Saturday, every two hours Sunday.

Parking: In the pub's car park. Roadside parking is possible but limited: try Swan Street nearby, between the High Street and the parish church.

Length of the walk: 5¼ miles. Map: OS Landranger 153 Bedford, Huntingdon and surrounding area (GR 267396).

Not far from Ashwell's marvellous High Street the walk joins a track heading for the summit of Newnham Hill, where there are outstanding views across nearby Bedfordshire and Cambridgeshire. The walk descends to medieval Hinxworth Place and returns to Ashwell across level fields and along quiet lanes.

The Walk
Turning left out of the Rose and Crown you will soon pass Bear House which has an interesting architectural feature: three glassed-over quatrefoils in the north-east corner. These acted as ventilators (without the glass, of course) for the food store in this 14th century hall-house.

Continuing along the High Street you may notice that it becomes West End before describing an S bend. When you meet Hinxworth Road branch right into this and, when it soon turns right, join a chalky track going straight on. After following the backs of gardens you will be launched into open country, with a hedge for company and a magnificent view across Bedfordshire and Cambridgeshire – and a little of Hertfordshire.

When the hedge bears left beyond the summit of the track, go with it downhill to a waymarked T-junction. Turn right here and follow another hedge downhill (300°) in the general direction of a distant water tower. Ignore a path going left when you are almost down to the lowest level and continue forward, with Hinxworth church coming into view directly ahead. By keeping straight on along a series of field edges, you will eventually (⅔ mile) pass between a long black timber barn and a garden. Soon after this a waymarked metal gate appears on the right. Prior to going through that gate a few yards in

115

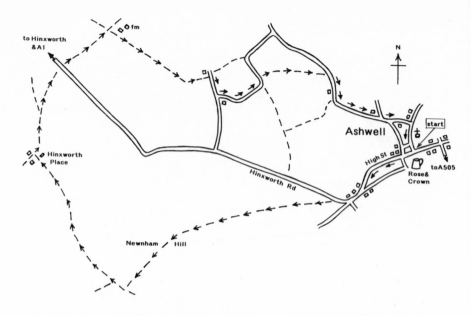

the opposite direction (left) will place you close to Hinxworth Place, thought to be one of the best-preserved stone manor houses in Hertfordshire. It was built in the 1400s with chalk stone quarried locally.

Go through the previously mentioned gate and follow a hedge for 30 yards to a waymark post at a hedge corner. Turn half-left from the hedge corner and strike across a very large field (10°). If a tiled-roof barn is directly behind you, you are on course! When you are almost halfway along the field a path might be apparent heading towards Hinxworth church: ignore this and continue straight on to another waymark post in a hedge corner, then straight on again following a hedge of sorts (with an interesting variety of trees) into the field's far left-hand corner, and on to a road.

Cross the road to a bridleway opposite (the drive to Arbtree Farm) and go along this for ¼ mile to a concreted area, near barns and about 50 yards before a pole-mounted transformer. Turn right here across the grass (120°), soon entering a field and continuing straight on, aiming at two light grey barns ⅔ mile away. A footbridge on the far side of this field places you on a path in a much smaller field, and this in turn leads you straight on to a narrow hedge gap and footbridge opposite. Go through the gap and into another field and turn left immediately, following the hedge to a lane at the field corner (70°).

Turn right in the lane and left at a T-junction, near those grey barns.

116

Passing The Oaks bungalow and farm (near the corner) stay with the lane to its second left bend. Ignore the bridleway sign in the corner and continue to the footpath sign on the right just around the corner. Go over the stile here and head across the field in the same direction as you walked the lane, passing about 20 yards to the right of an electricity pole (60° initially). The path curves right a little as it crosses the field, and heads towards barns (dark grey this time) joining a lane from a stile – a few yards right of a hedge gap. Ashwell's parish church has now come into view and is looking good: and so it should, having the highest tower in Hertfordshire.

On leaving the field turn right in the lane and go left with it by a fruit farm. Continue forward at a road junction, and forward again into Rollys Lane, where you have a view of Ashwell Bury beyond the pasture on the left. From the end of the lane turn right into Mill Street (or left to see the mill and its wheels, and the river) and pass between the church and the Bushel and Strike pub.

The church is certainly worth more than a passing glance. What are referred to as the Graffiti Scratchings can be seen on the inside tower wall. They include a drawing of Old St Paul's before the Great Fire of London in 1666; also inscriptions relating to the Plague of 1349–50 and the Great Storm of 1362.

At the top of Mill Street lies Swan Street and the fine timber-framed building housing Ashwell's museum, and to the right of this a lovely cottage garden maintained by the villagers, who successfully fought off an attempt to build here. Passing the garden and turning left out of Swan Street into Gardiners Lane, glance back at the unusual chalk wall – complete with thatch.

Your day will not be complete without walking the length of the High Street eastward – at least as far as The Springs. The river Rhee is fed from this attractive spot, which (according to the information board there) accounts for an average of 1.3 million gallons a day.

Therfield
The Fox and Duck

Once you have visited the Fox and Duck you will understand why it is so popular. The selection of fine ales – including five real ales – is certainly one of the pub's attractions. Equal to this is the wide range of snacks and meals – very nicely prepared and available every lunchtime and evening except Sunday evening (11 am to 2 pm and 7 pm to 10 pm Monday to Saturday, 12 noon to 2 pm Sunday). If you have brought your own food and intend to purchase drinks you may dine in the garden or, if it's raining, in the small porch at the front. Walking parties are made very welcome, but they usually give warning that they are coming. Children having meals are also welcome inside and dogs may be taken into the bar if kept on a lead.

The pub is open for drinking all day (11 am to 11 pm) on Saturdays all year round. Opening times on other days are normal. Bed and breakfast accommodation is available.

Telephone: 01763 87246.

How to get there: The pub overlooks the green at Therfield and is not far from the parish church. Therfield is signposted from the A10(T) 2½ miles south of Royston. A transport café marks the spot. It is also signposted from the A505 between Royston and Baldock. The A10(T) is the nearest main road to Therfield.

Parking: In the pub's car park or alongside the green.

Length of the walk: 3½ miles. Map: OS Landranger 153 Bedford, Huntingdon and surrounding area, and 154 Cambridge, Newmarket and surrounding area (GR 336373).

What better place to start and finish a walk than at one of Hertfordshire's best-kept small villages? From the precincts of Therfield's church the walk very nearly describes a figure of eight centred on the peaceful hamlet of Kelshall, where there is a fine church and rectory and an attractive main street.

The Walk

From the Fox and Duck cross the green to Church Lane opposite. This lane is signposted 'Church Only' and soon terminates at the churchyard gate. Passing to the left of the church go through a metal gate opposite the porch and continue in the same direction but just outside the churchyard. When a branch goes off to the water tower keep straight on along two field edges in succession (260°). These field edges are linked by a small footbridge and end at a road by The Gables, a thatched cottage.

Turn left in the road and, passing a pond on the right, go along to a road junction beyond the 'Kelshall National School 1895' – now Kelshall's village hall. On the right-hand corner stands a reminder of better times – the Old Crown! And the stone at the centre of the little triangular green is all that remains of a village cross. It was found in 1906 and installed here, although it may well date from the 1300s.

Continue forward a little and join the drive on the left labelled 'Church Only – No Through Road'. You will see part of the Old Rectory beyond the hedge before turning right with the drive, and when you reach the end of the drive you will find a signpost near Church Cottage, opposite the churchyard gate. Enter the fenced field from the signpost and aim for a stile in the fence to the right of a pond, near the field's far right-hand corner. Go over this and forward to the outer corner of the fence, then walk half-right (assuming your back is to the church) across a field towards a gap between a few tall trees (200° and not necessarily according to the waymark arrow on the fence).

From a stile in that corner there are two further fields to cross, almost in the same direction as previously (220°) and interrupted by a bridleway crossing. If in doubt aim for the distant field corner, slightly right of farm buildings. The exit from the field corner is by a ditch and connects with a road.

Turn left in the road and go along to a 'Public Byway' (70 yards) on the left just beyond Woodcotes. This will take you along a grassy track

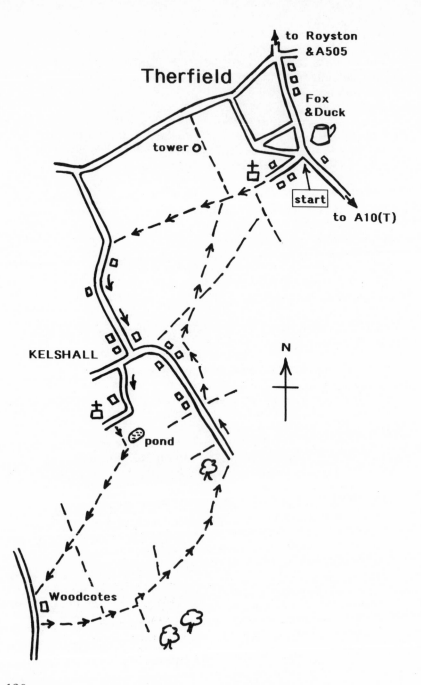

Therfield

to Royston
&A505

Fox
&Duck

tower o

start

to A10(T)

KELSHALL

pond

N

Woodcotes

between the house (and its hedge) and a field. Stay with the hedge for ⅓ mile, passing a left branching bridleway to Kelshall beyond the halfway point and finally meeting up with a track coming in from the right. Go forward and downhill in the track and follow it for ½ mile to its T-junction with another track, ignoring a footpath leaving from the left on the way. Turning left at the junction and passing some of the cottages (you are now back in Kelshall) look for a footpath signpost and stile on the right almost opposite Chippins.

Cross the field here in the direction of the left-hand finger of the signpost – i.e. half-left if standing with your back to the road (10°). This will take you to the right of a pond and to a stile in the adjacent hedge. From the near corner of the next field go along its left-hand edge following a fence and parallel to the houses (330°), then straight on across a protrusion in the field to the same field's far left-hand corner – where there is a waymark post and a footbridge.

On entry to the next field you may find that the path has not been reinstated after ploughing or planting. If this is so you will need to take courage and cross the field in the direction of Therfield's church (20°). This will take you to a bridge linking this field to the next. Taking your cue from the left-branching waymark arrow at the bridge, walk across the next field by aiming at a point midway between church and water tower (10°). After passing through a hedge gap into yet another field, cross this to a hedge corner, aiming a little left of the church. On arrival at the corner turn right and make your way back to the church and village.

29 Barkway
The Tally Ho

What may strike you most of all when you enter the Tally Ho are the very reasonable food prices. These are by no means at the expense of quality, quantity or presentation, each of which is exemplary. The regular food menu covers virtually the whole range of pub fare including rolls and sandwiches, burgers, ploughman's, filled jacket potatoes, omelettes and an all day breakfast. The daily specials blackboard menu lists a goodly number of main meals, ranging from about three vegetarian dishes at one end of the spectrum to the popular very large mixed grill at the other. Both menus are available every lunchtime (12 noon to 2.30 pm) and evening. This includes Sunday evenings, but in summertime only.

Normal drinking hours are kept, except on summer Saturdays, when the pub is open from 11 am until 11 pm. And if it's a warm sunny Saturday, that's a good time to be in the garden enjoying one of the three real ales, Greene King IPA and Abbot Ale, and XX Dark Mild. Children are welcome in the dining-room if having meals. Dogs can only be taken into the bar or the garden.

Telephone: 01763 848389.

How to get there: If coming via the A10(T), take the road from Buckland (midway between Buntingford and Royston) signposted to Barkway. This 1½ mile road will take you direct to the Tally Ho, which is situated at the southern end of Barkway's High Street.

Parking: In the pub's car park or along the High Street.

Length of the walk: 5 miles. Map: OS Landranger 154 Cambridge, Newmarket and surrounding area (GR 384349).

For an appreciation of some of Hertfordshire's finest domestic buildings, this walk follows the entire length of Barkway's High Street, after which it strikes across country to Reed and its well-known pub, the Cabinet. Although Reed is one of the highest villages in the county, the walk is level and uncomplicated, with absolutely no stiles to slow you down.

The Walk

On leaving the Tally Ho turn right into the High Street (which looks very unlike a High Street at this point) and walk its entire length to the Chaise and Pair pub and the war memorial. Turn left in the road here (signposted to Reed), and when this soon turns right go forward into a public byway (ignoring a footpath branching to the left). After 400 yards the route divides at a fork in a shallow dip in the fields.

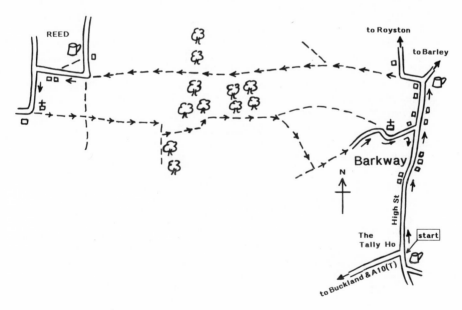

123

Ignore the right-hand branch (which follows a ditch and aims at an aerial mast) and keep forward along the main track by following a hedge on the left.

The track eventually runs alongside a wood on the left, and then continues straight on as a wide track between fields. It heads for a gap between the trees before passing under electricity wires and crossing more fields. Houses and barns come into view half-right as you cross these fields, and then the track continues forward between hedges and trees. When you come to another track at a T-junction, turn right to join Reed's High Street (just a quiet country lane) at a road corner and in sight of the Cabinet public house.

Unless you have an inclination to explore the Cabinet (a well placed halfway house) you should turn left at the corner and follow the road to a T-junction, passing a very fine farmhouse on the way. Turn left at the T-junction into a road signposted to the church, then leave the road when it turns right and go into the churchyard. Passing to the right of the church you may take advantage of the churchyard seat (as I usually do!) before making your return journey to Barkway.

Continuing in line with the south wall of the church go through a gap in the churchyard hedge and strike across a field, aiming for a point at the far end about ⅓ of the way from the left-hand corner (90°). You may find a footbridge at this point to take you straight on across a ditch and into the next field; but if this is not in place you will need to circulate clockwise around the field edges (a short distance only) in order to meet the continuation of the path on the opposite side of the ditch. Once there you should resume your previous direction (90°), crossing the field towards a thin line of tall trees (viewed end on). As a check on your position you should be walking along a straight line between the church and those trees.

Walk the length of that line of trees (trees on your left) into the field corner. Turn right from that corner and follow a hedge on the left until you reach the right-hand extremity of a wood ahead (200 yards). Although the track continues straight on you will need to turn left in another track (80°) so that the wood is on your right.

This will take you along the right-hand edge of another wood and, when the wood terminates, into a left-hand turn. This is soon followed by a right-hand turn, which returns you to your previous direction. Barkway church and village come into view ahead as you cross more fields and as you make your way along the right-hand edge of yet another wood.

After leaving the wood edge the track crosses fields again before following a hedge on the left and arriving at what is in effect a T-junction. Go left with the track and stay with it to Barkway's church and the High Street, turning right there for the Tally Ho.

30 Barley
The Fox and Hounds

As a building the Fox and Hounds dates back to about 1450. It became an alehouse at a very early time and was licensed in 1790 as the Wagon and Horses. It took on its present mantle when the original Fox and Hounds (sited elsewhere in the village) was burnt down. The pub is certainly unusual in the way its sign spans the road.

The Fox and Hounds is a drinker's pub par excellence, with about 100 different beers gracing the bar in the course of a year! And as if that isn't enough the pub has its own brewery on site. Nathaniel's Special takes pride of place here, with other varieties being brewed from time to time. It is also interesting to find something out of the ordinary in the way of traditional ciders. The two varieties on offer are Thatcher's and Biddenden, both certainly worth a try. Drinking hours are normal.

Drink is not the only speciality at the Fox and Hounds: I counted 66 items on the blackboard menu. This vast choice is available lunchtimes and evenings seven days a week. In addition there is a lunchtime snack menu every day, but limited to cold items on Sundays. Children are very welcome, either in the side room or in the dining-room.

Telephone: 01763 848459.

How to get there: The pub is in the centre of Barley at a sharp bend in the B1368. It can be approached from Royston along the B1039 followed by the B1368 (3 miles).

Parking: In the pub's car park or by the parish church in Church End.

Length of the walk: 3½ miles. Map: OS Landranger 154 Cambridge, Newmarket and surrounding area (GR 400384).

A walk with wide sweeping views typical of North Hertfordshire, mellowed by the woodlands of Newsells Park and the beautifully kept cottages at Smith's End.

The Walk

From the front door of the Fox and Hounds step forward into London Road in the Barkway and Hare Street direction and go along this to a branch on the right – The Mount – just before the Chequers pub. This branch is effectively straight on and soon passes to the right of Mount House (and other houses) before evolving from a road to a track. Follow this downhill to the bottom of a wide valley and turn left into a sandy track. A 'Private' notice will then be behind you and paddocks on your right.

After you cross a very superior drive and continue straight on, you will pass between hedges along a more conventional track. The track becomes a road by Fox Cottage and terminates at a three-way road junction. Your next move is to climb the bank to the left of a rough-hewn memorial stone, but if you take delight in old thatched cottages, there are four immaculate specimens to be seen along the road ahead. These are within the approaches to Newsells Park, a house burnt down in the Second World War and rebuilt in Georgian style in 1954.

Having climbed that bank in the direction of the signpost finger (90°), you will soon be walking just inside a wood. The path comes briefly out into the open at the top of the hill, giving an equally brief view over the paddocks. It crosses a drive here and resumes its passage under the trees. When you come out into the open at the bottom of the hill go half-right to a stile.

The next stage is to cross the field ahead to a stile on the opposite side, more or less maintaining your previous direction (60°); but for those not entirely fearless when it comes to entering fields where there are horses, an alternative route is signposted. This encircles the field anticlockwise and ends up in the same place – but will add ¼ mile to your walk. Whatever your inclination two more stiles will place you on a road, where you should turn left. Follow the road down to a footpath sign on the right, where the road begins to ascend. Cross the ditch here (planks are provided) and strike across the field

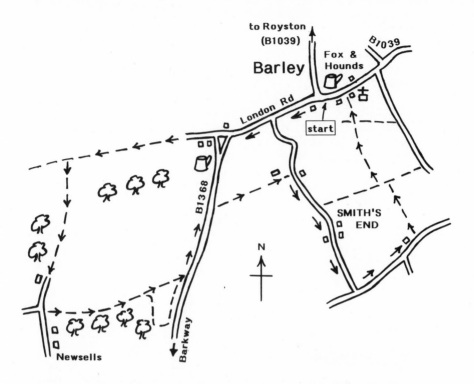

towards its summit (65°), eventually meeting up with a terrace of three cottages. You may well find that the path is obliterated by crops. If this is the case you should if possible keep to the prescribed route – and have the satisfaction of helping those who follow.

From the cottages pass to the left of a black metal barn and join a road. You could now call it a day by turning left here for Barley (⅓ mile), but in so doing you will miss the delightful hamlet of Smith's End, as well as some good views thereafter. Assuming you are persuaded, turn right and walk through the hamlet (⅓ mile) to a T-junction. Turn left there (Nuthampstead direction) and go downhill to a track on the left signposted 'Barley ½' 60 yards beyond the next road junction.

When this uphill track goes left to a paddock, continue forward along a footpath, following power lines and enjoying the view – which includes Chishill's windmill ¾ mile over to your right. And when confronted by a hedge at a T-junction in the path, turn left and go over a stile in the hedge after a few yards. Then resume your previous direction by crossing a pasture and aiming for a wooden electricity pole where wires branch three ways. Go over a stile just

127

beyond the pole and keep forward between hedges, ignoring a kissing-gate on the right and continuing in the main path to Church End, Barley.

Across the road from the church is the very fine Tudor Town House built in about 1530; it is now the village hall. It has a varied history, including (or so it is said) courthouse, workhouse, almshouse and school. At the road junction opposite the Fox and Hounds the 17th century lock up or cage was used for the temporary detention of suspected lawbreakers and drunks – very conveniently placed for the pub!